A House Deconstructed

OFFICE OF (UN)CERTAINTY RESEARCH

Mark Jarzombek + Vikramaditya Prakash

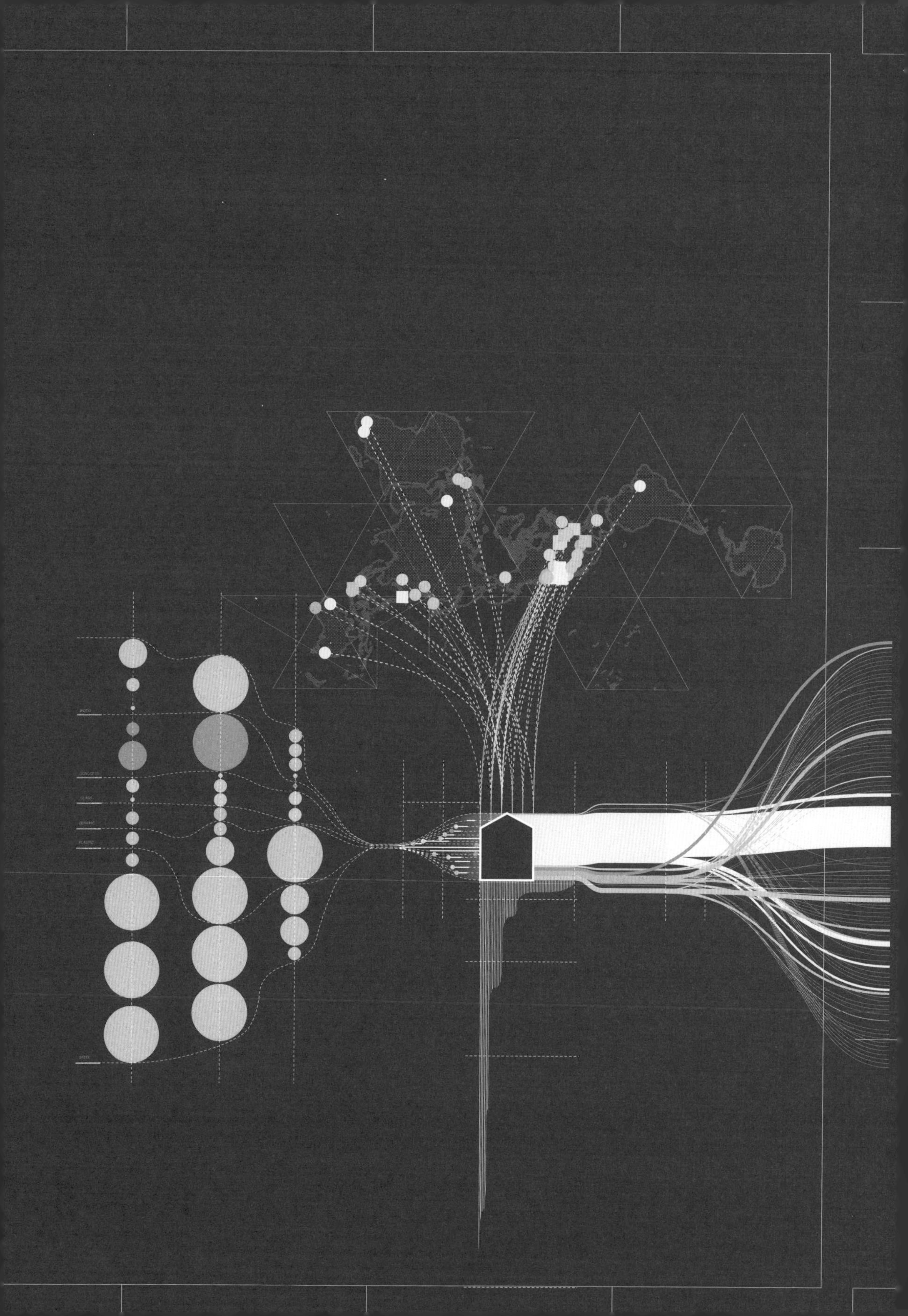

A House Deconstructed

A planetary meditation on architecture

by

Mark Jarzombek + Vikramaditya Prakash

OFFICE OF (UN)CERTAINTY RESEARCH

OUR: Office of (Un)Certainty Research is a design research practice dedicated to rethinking architecture in terms of the emergent scientific, social and political parameters of the 21st century.

For OUR students, past, present and future.

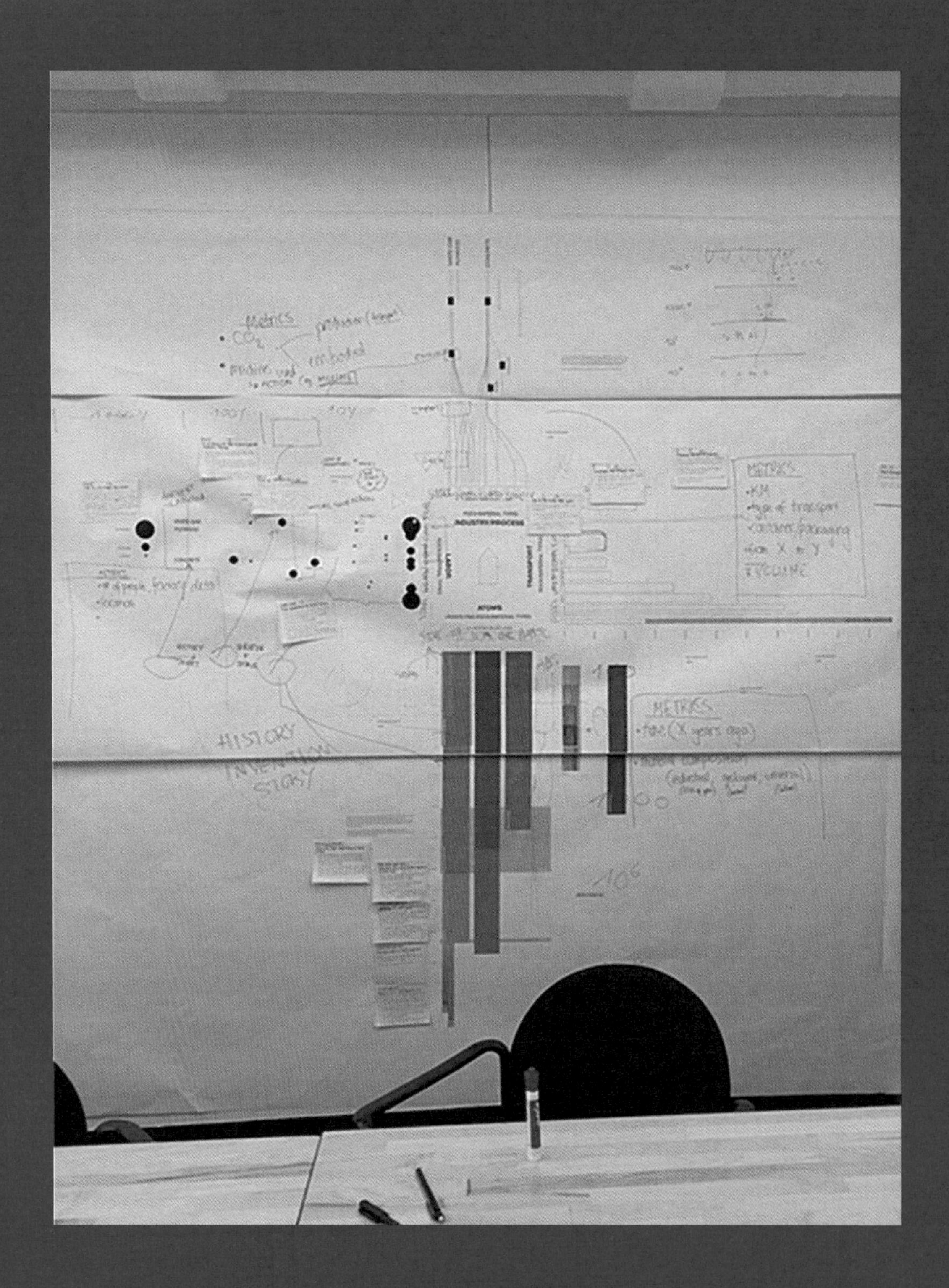

+ *A classroom at MIT during the spring of 2020 with notes on a mock-up diagram in a photo by Olivier Faber.*

A House Deconstructed

research contributors

Research Assistant + Book Editor

Angie Door

Exhibition Art Director

Paul Montie

Researchers

Ana Arenas

Angela Loescher-Montal

Ardalan SadeghiKivi

Arditha Auriyane

Daisy Zhang

Kailin Jones

Melika Konjicanin

Natasha Hirt

Olivier Faber

Sacha Moreau

Sanjana Lahiri

Thaddeus Lee

We would like to thank Allied8 of Seattle, the architects of the house, for their ongoing support of this project. This publication was generously supported by grants from the Office of the Dean, MIT School of Architecture and Planning, and the Office of Research, College of Built Environments, University of Washington via the Johnson-Hastings Publications Support Fund.

Index

Index

Index

Index

Positions + Exhibition

Positions + Exhibition

A House

1119 25th Avenue East
Seattle, WA 98112
United States

1,080 sq. ft.
Date of Construction: 2018

The architects designed a three-room addition to an existing house in a modernist idiom. They sought to maximize access to light and the outdoors, while taking advantage of the steep slope to tuck an additional room into the hill. Low maintenance metal siding defines the exterior, while generously sized windows offer interconnections between the living space and the partially enclosed yard.

\+ A photo of the house by Allied8 architects.

A House Deconstructed:
A planetary meditation on architecture

The Office of (Un)Certainty Research (OUR) studied a single, modest, modernist house located in Seattle, Washington, USA.

A house is like a black hole.

It draws a huge amount of energy, creativity, materials, labor, and molecules into its orbit. But in the end what does it tell us? The decisiveness of the final building—its gravitational hold on the earth—belies the tangled web of realities that made it happen. For that reason, we need to remind ourselves of the strange inversion in play when we take on the study of a building's history, even one as small as a single-family home. While the very idea of architectural "re-search" promises the possibility of intelligibility, a house—as a signifier of architecture—seeks to preserve the secret that is at the discipline's core and indeed at the core of modernity: the violence of the productivity that makes this house possible. The Office of (Un)Certainty Research (OUR) focused on a single, modest, modernist house located in Seattle, Washington, USA.

The house serves as an agent of modernism, which seeks its affirmation in the upper registers of abstraction. Its clean lines signify rationality, professionalism and transparency. But these same clean lines suppress information and complications regarding the history of the materials before they arrived onsite. That is, the history of the house's modernity is also the history of modernity's cover-up of the uncertain and at times unsightly realities of the world.

In spite of its self-presentation as firmly embedded to the earth, architecture is in fact globally (un)moored and constiutively entangled with our planet's history and future. A single modern house reaches around the planet in dimensions that are social, economic, ecological, political, and even interstellar, stretching into the domain of the history of our universe. But the house, like all architecture, is designed to cover over all of this, in the interests of aesthetics and use, its normatizing silence a barrier to a fuller epistemological and disciplinary critique.

What, then, is the backstory of this Seattle house? Most architects might think they know to the answers, but in truth, most are just as ignorant as the general population. Their job is to deliver a persuasive product, not to interrogate its deep onto-epistemic pre-history.

To enter into the contradictions of the architectural object, OUR researched this solitary, small house as a portal to better locate, describe, and understand architecture's indeterminate place on the earth and its planetary origins and impact.

\+ *A photo of the house by Allied8 architects.*

We researched the house along four registers, each a type of consciousness that is silenced once the owners receive the keys to the front door:

Atomic Consciousness

extending back to the Big Bang and the earliest supernovas

Production Consciousness

a vast array of ingredients to make architectural products

Labor Consciousness

multilayered and global in reach

Source Consciousness

digging into the earth and chopping the forests

Each of these has powerful stories to tell.

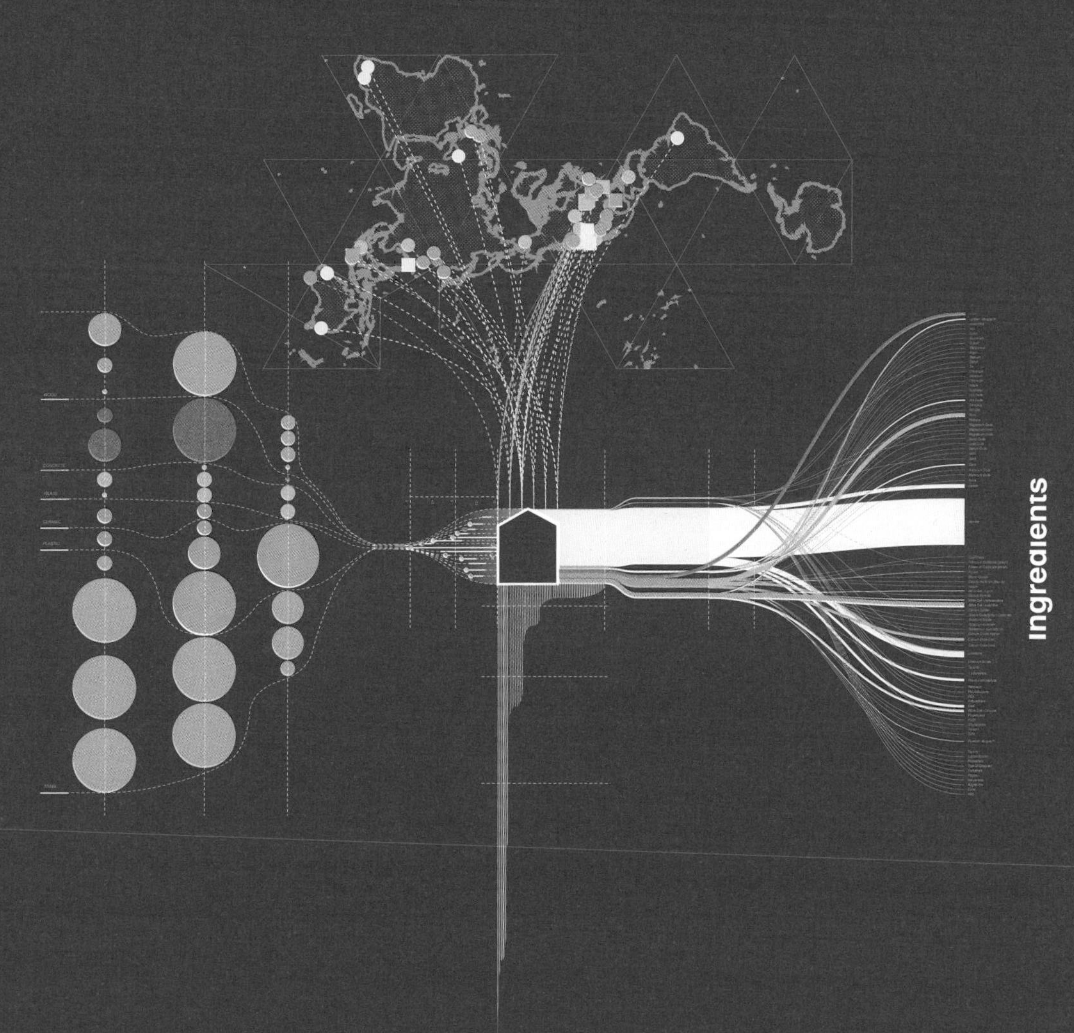
Sources
Labors
Ingredients
Atoms

The global nature of the house-making enterprise quickly became clear when we indexed the sources of its materials. The wood, for instance, was about one hundred years old and harvested from forests in south Germany. The iron, like other heavy metals, was produced in stars and distributed into deep space when they collapsed and went supernova; the iron made its way to Earth as a part of the process of our solar system's formation and via asteroids some 4.5 billion years ago. At the other end of the temporal spectrum is the dramatic escalation in complexity of industrial systems of material production during the last twenty years.

From that perspective, the modernism of this house is far different from the modernism of even some thirty years ago. Since then, we have seen a quiet revolution of the building industry involving metallification (the house's rebars, siding, railings, beams, all rendered cheap in the neoliberal economy), plastification (in the house's piping and the coating on the steel), chemicalization (in the glues, additives, laminants, and insulation), and computationalization (in the design, production, and assembly).

The recycled steel that was celebrated as such by the suppliers who delivered the beams to the house probably came through Chitagong, Bangladesh, where discarded ships are cut up by the hundreds, releasing toxic chemicals and gases, while workers are paid almost nothing and are uncompensated for injuries.

\+ *A photo of the house under construction by Vikramaditya Prakash.*

Some parts of stories like these are rendered invisible by the calculated manipulations of capital; others by the inadequacies of documentation (purposeful or not); and others still by the core uncertainty of any attempt to trace the processes of production and labor.

Thus, even though we pushed this research to the level of the granular, we want to emphasize the following attributes of architectural supply:

- the indeterminate status of the architectural object.

- the existence of both proximate and non-proximate relationships.

- the positive impossibility of comprehension across scales.

In sum, one could say that habitation in today's world is shot through with unavoidable distances and indifferences; yet habitation does not thereby cease to be a mode of belonging even if architecture protects its sense of purposefulness by means of its silencing mechanisms. Our questions are: How do we define and measure our response and responsibility? And how can we imagine a different way of teaching, learning about, and building architecture—indeed a new form of architectural agency for the future.

A photo of the house under construction by Vikramaditya Prakash.

Deconstructing the architectural object is akin to quantum research. The closer you look, the more things become uncertain, not because our instruments are not strong enough or calibrated precisely enough, but because things themselves are indeterminate and uncertain.

Holistically speaking, knowledge tends to the indeterminate, constitutively entangled with our modality of looking. This is certainly true of subatomic particles, of which all architecture is ultimately made, but it is also true of the geographic sources of things, the processes that manufacture materials, and the laborers who are engaged in the production of work.

Is the house a familiar object or a foreign object? From the point of view of the architect, contractor, and student of architecture, and even the client, it is familiar. But from its own position as modern—and indeed as architecture—it is of necessity foreign, belonging to a different planet than the one that it seems to sit upon.

A photo of the house under construction by Vikramaditya Prakash.

There is no Archimedean point by which one can understand the modernity of architecture. Not in the history of its aesthetics, materials, labor, or even in its self-professed critiques. And yet a building as it stands in the landscape is not a contradiction. On the contrary, it speaks unambiguously. But about what? The more one studies the house—or better yet—fights against its foreclosures, the more one realizes it has an almost magical place in contemporary culture. But if in one breath it is magical, in the next it is scandalous.

We think we are designers—authors of note—with agency. But our agency is truly circumscribed, emplaced and enabled by a complex prehistory that spans millions of years, engages an array of industrial processes, complex social and civilizational forces, and puts the earth into play in ways that are well beyond quotidian apprehension. Architectural agency is a circumscribed chimera, powerful in some respects, and deeply indebted and weighted in others.

+ *A photo of the house under construction by Vikramaditya Prakash.*

"Institutions in culture must precomprehend [. . . the] instituting of culture, not simply as a chronologically prior event but as a philosophically subtending layer."

— Gayatri Chakravorty Spivak

The architect is the ‘grammatical subject’ of architecture, but there is no intervening verb. Thus the magic. Thus the impossibility of finding ‘theory’ outside of play of words.

— O(U)R

How is one to measure the full impact of architecture? While the various metrices that measure the carbon impact of buildings have significantly sharpened our understanding of the broad impact of construction and construction materials, these measures are designed to generate practicable metrics useful for comparing one building to another—oranges to oranges. While this is of course very useful and important, a more detailed examination of the ultimate sources and impacts of architecture—of the detailed origins, labors, and distances of materials—poses a formidable challenge and can generate complexities and distances that boggle the mind.

Construction materials across the board have undergone an Additive Revolution during the past twenty years. Additives have made materials stronger, more durable, and cheaper, in various combinations. This chemicalization of materials has, however, opened up a host of problems completely invisible to the public—and even to the architect—regarding planetary exploitation.

Structural steel, for instance, is an alloy of over 16 metals, each with its own history and sources that involve multiple mines, transports, and labors that are spread across distant nations and economic entities. Just the thin casing that covers a standard metal rod, for example, is a petroleum product that can originate in the Middle East, be manufactured in the central United States, then shipped to Australia, where it is applied to the manufactured steel rods, before those rods are shipped back to Los Angeles, from where they may be trucked to Seattle for installation.

The question, therefore, ought not to be: How does one describe architecture? Rather, it should be: How does architecture describe the world?

The sheer globality of this enterprise becomes mind-bending when we try to index the deep sources of materials. Wood for instance can be just about twenty years old, and locally harvested. But iron, like other heavy metals, was almost entirely created in exploding stars, that formed the dust cloud from which first our sun and then the rest of the solar system was created about 4.5 billion years ago. As the earth congealed the heavier metals sunk down to the core, from where they were, and continue to be, periodically redistributed up to the surface through geological activity, which makes it accessible to us.

+ *A photo of the house under construction by Vikramaditya Prakash.*

Michael Burawoy is a professor at the University of California, Berkeley. He has been a participant observer of industrial workplaces in Zambia, the United States, Hungary, and Russia. In his different projects he analyzes postcolonialism, capitalism, class consciousness and work organizations developing a methodology that is advanced in Global Ethnography, a book coauthored with nine graduate students, that shows how globalization can be studied “from below” through participating in the lives of those who experience it.

"We begin with global forces. We draw on all sorts of secondary constructions to create a picture of the 'global' economy, polity, and culture as composed of forces constituted beyond our sites. The global force makes itself felt through mediators that transmit it as their interest or as the subjective internalization of values or beliefs. The locality in turn can fight back, adapt, or simply be destroyed [...]. [Global] movement is manifold and multiple, combined and reversible, uneven and unpredictable. We, therefore, work [...] ascending from the local to the global by stitching together our ethnographies. But this has its problems too. It cannot be done tabula rasa. We needed an orienting map that is attentive to both global and local simultaneously, that would allow us to compose the global from below. It had to be a vision that identified what was new about globalization against the skeptics, but without surrendering to the totalizing mode of the radicals."

Michael Burawoy, Joseph A. Blum, Sheba Mariam George, Zsuzsa Gille, and Millie Thayer, Global Ethnography: Forces, Connections, and Imaginations in a Postmodern World (Berkeley, CA: Berkeley University Press, 2000).

O(U)R research station: *Many Houses Many Worlds* (out of competition) at the Biennale Architecttura 2020, HOW WILL WE LIVE TOGETHER? curated by Hashim Sarkis.

Hashim Sarkis invited OUR to present a research station at the 2020 architecture biennnale in Venice. Exhibited with an interactive interface of the Global Architectural History Teaching Collaborative - GAHTC, A House Deconstructed constitued a pair entitled “Many Houses, Many Worlds”.

Our diagram highlighting the four vectors was centered approximately at the human eye level. We hoped that visitors would leave with the disturbing thought that even a small building has a huge global and planetary footprint. We wanted visitors to get a sense of the deep history of materials that goes back in time many billions of years.

Our installation sought to draw in visitors from a distance based on the overall lucidity of the diagram, and offered a depth of information for those who inspected it up close.

The following text is from the catalog of the biennale:

“Architecture today is addicted to four basic products: steel, concrete, glass, and plastic. Each is a figure in the hyper-industrial world in which we live. We are living in the golden age of the Quadrivium Industrial Complex. Though imagined as elements of modernity, it was only with the neo-liberal economy with the 1990s and the consolidation of the construction industries that these materials could be normalized. The result: never in human history has mining, production, delivery and assembly - the basic activities of the Quadrivium Industrial Complex - been more extensive and cheaper. Yet this golden age will not last forever. What is its future?

What is the backstory of this house? Even the architects themselves might not even know.

A house is like a Black Hole. It sucks a huge amount of energy, creativity, materials, labor and molecules into its orbit. But in the end what does the house tell us about all of that. Nothing.

Habitation in today’s world is shot through with unavoidable distances and indifferences; yet it does not thereby cease to be a mode of belonging. The question is: How do we define/measure our response/ responsibility?”

\+ A House Deconstructed *exhibition photo by Office of (Un)Certainty Research.*

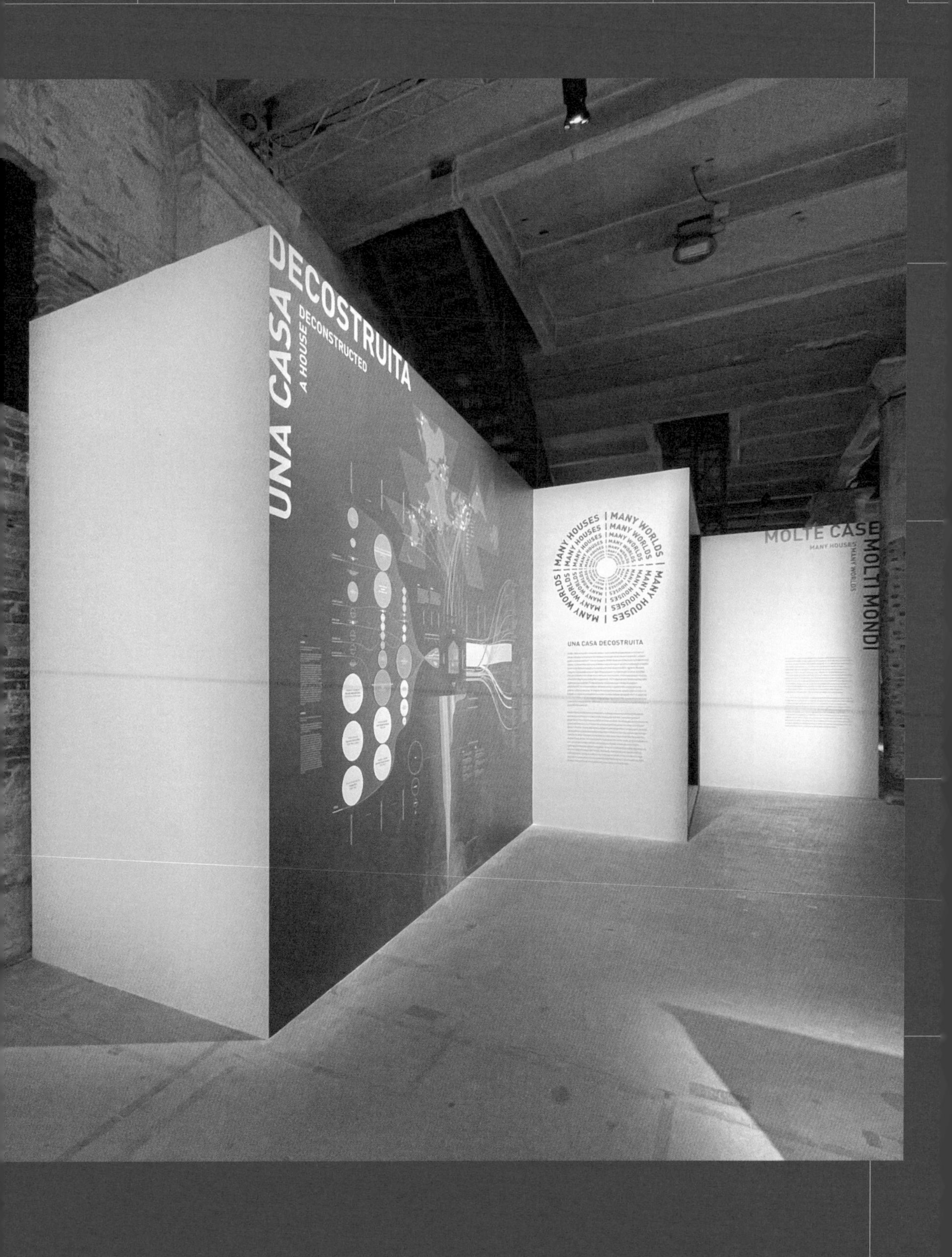
UNA CASA DECOSTRUITA
A HOUSE DECONSTRUCTED
MANY HOUSES | MANY WORLDS
UNA CASA DECOSTRUITA
MOLTE CASE
MANY HOUSES
MOLTI MONDI
MANY WORLDS

UNA CASA DECOSTRUITA
A HOUSE DECONSTRUCTED
MANY HOUSES | MANY WORLDS
UNA CASA DECOSTRUITA

+ *The exhibition in a photo by Office of (Un)Certainty Research.*

+ The exhibition in a photo by Office of (Un)Certainty Research.

MANY HOUSES | MANY WORLDS
MOLTI MONDI
MANY HOUSES
MANY WORLDS
Among
Diverse Beings

Ingredients

Ingredients

Ingredients

Production consciousness— combining a vast array of ingredients to make architectural products

Before WWII, and well into the 1980s, a modern-styled house would have had little steel and almost no plastic. The plumbing would have been made of cast iron and copper tubing. Single pane windows did not require double-glazing and there was limited use of caulking. The prime use of oil was in the form of asphalt shingles which made their appearance in the 1920s and 1930s.

Since the 1980s, the "ingredient list" for a standard modern house has grown dramatically. It also now contains some of the most toxic chemicals on the planet, as well as chemicals that are at the apex of the industrial production system, especially those involved in the making of plastic.

On the left-hand side of the graph are the conventional designators of materials: Wood, Concrete, Plastic, Steel, etc. On the right their elemental origins. A ton of "concrete," for instance, is more than just sand, gravel, and mortar, but also has a host of additives, most of which are unknown to anyone but specialists in the field. Additives—which have become increasingly numerous in the last twenty years—have extended the reach of building materials into the vastness of global, capitalist geography through sourcing and production.

How an elemental ingredient is transmuted into a dull semiotic is not only a triumph of chemical engineering, it is also a large part of the "magic" of architecture.

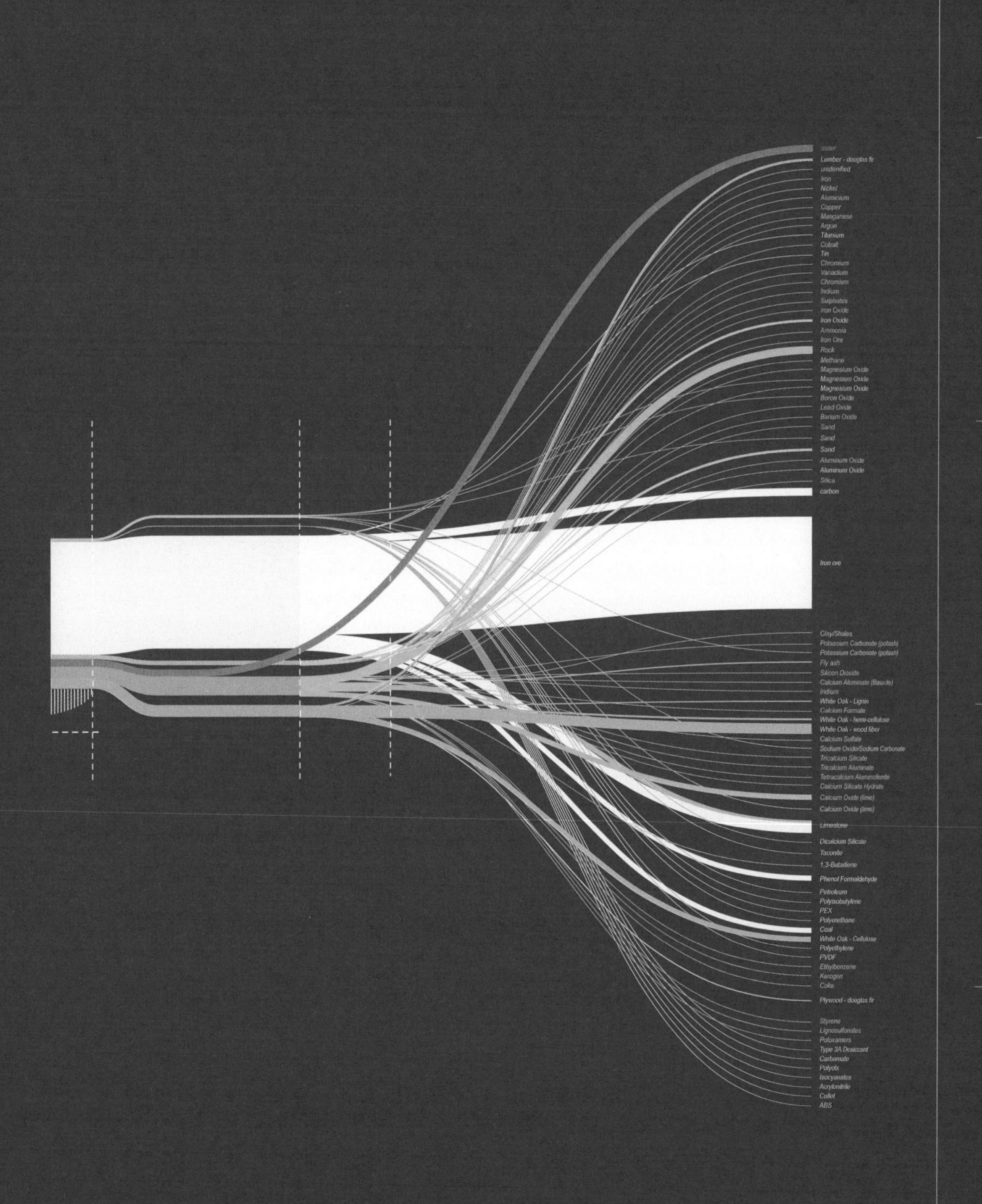
water
Lumber - douglas fir
unidenified
Iron
Nickel
Aluminium
Copper
Manganese
Argon
Titanium
Cobalt
Tin
Chromium
Vanadium
Chromium
Indium
Sulphates
Iron Oxide
Iron Oxide
Ammonia
Iron Ore
Rock
Methane
Magnesium Oxide
Magnesium Oxide
Magnesium Oxide
Boron Oxide
Lead Oxide
Barium Oxide
Sand
Sand
Sand
Aluminum Oxide
Aluminum Oxide
Silica
carbon
Iron ore
Clay/Shales
Potassium Carbonate (potash)
Potassium Carbonate (potash)
Fly ash
Silicon Dioxide
Calcium Aluminate (Bauxite)
Indium
White Oak - Lignin
Calcium Formate
White Oak - hemi-cellulose
White Oak - wood fiber
Calcium Sulfate
Sodium Oxide/Sodium Carbonate
Tricalcium Silicate
Tricalcium Aluminate
Tetracalcium Aluminoferrite
Calcium Silicate Hydrate
Calcium Oxide (lime)
Calcium Oxide (lime)
Limestone
Dicalcium Silicate
Taconite
1,3-Butadiene
Phenol Formaldehyde
Petroleum
Polyisobutylene
PEX
Polyurethane
Coal
White Oak - Cellulose
Polyethylene
PVDF
Ethylbenzene
Kerogen
Coke
Plywood - douglas fir
Styrene
Lignosulfonates
Poloxamers
Type 3A Desiccant
Carbamate
Polyols
Isocyanates
Acrylonitrile
Cullet
ABS

Ovid, Metamorphosis
(c.8 CE)

“There is nothing in all the world that keeps its form. All things are in a state of flux, and everything is brought into being with a changing nature.”

Mireille Mazard discusses Nusu animism as practiced in villages in southwest China. See Mireille Mazard, "The Algebra of Souls: Ontological Multiplicity and the Transformation of Animism in Southwest China," Social Analysis: The International Journal of Anthropology *60 no. 1 (2016), 18–36. Mazard received her doctorate in anthropology from the University of Cambridge in 2011. Since then she has taught anthropology and gender studies in Pnom Penh, Cambodia, and Saskatchewan, Canada.*

"Rather than being a [normative] monadic individual, or even a relational individual, a person can, under certain conditions, evince different aspects of the self, with multiple ontological identities. Seen from another perspective, ontologically different persons can converge into one identity. […] An algebraic equation, static on the page, illustrates the movement and transformation of terms. Nusu personhood is reckoned complexly, as in algebra. Some of its attributes remain unknown or possibly in flux, while ontological shifts may bring unresolved elements to the fore."

“The ‘algebra of souls’ describes a socio-cosmic order in which personhood is subject to plurality and fragmentation. Unknown aspects continuously emerge from and propel the person throughout her or his lifetime, engaging visible and invisible aspects of self.”

WHAT IF ONE REPLACED ‘PERSONHOOD’ WITH ‘CHEMICALHOOD’, ‘SELF’ WITH ‘SELVES’?

Glass

The Seattle house features 316 square feet of glass in both existing as well as new windows and doors (the house we are discussing was an addition to an existing structure). As with most buildings, the glass used is categorized as soda-lime glass. As its name suggests, the key ingredients of this glass—in addition to sand (or silica, SiO_2)—are soda, or sodium carbonate (Na_2CO_3), and lime, which is also known as calcium oxide (CaO). These are typically mixed in at specific ratios depending on the desired qualities of glass, but glass roughly consists of 67% silicon dioxide/sand, 12% sodium oxide, and 10% calcium oxide by mass.

The three basic ingredients for glass have remained virtually unchanged for thousands of years, with the earliest known examples dating back to ancient Egypt (c.3000 BCE), and clear instructions for its manufacture recorded by the Assyrians in the 7th century BCE. But today's glass is nothing like glass of old. Not only is it much more precise in the proportioning of its core ingredients, it also contains a host of new fluxes, stabilizers, and opacifiers.These are added to the glass mixture to increase its chemical resistance, alter its mechanical properties, and to adjust its optical qualities, such as opacity or degree of refraction. Sulphates, calcium, magnesium, aluminum, iron and lead oxides are but some of the common chemicals added to modern glass. All these ingredients are mixed together in what is called a "batch," and melted in an industrial furnace at temperatures of over 2900°F (1600°C).

\+ *A glass window in the house in a photo by Allied8 architects.*

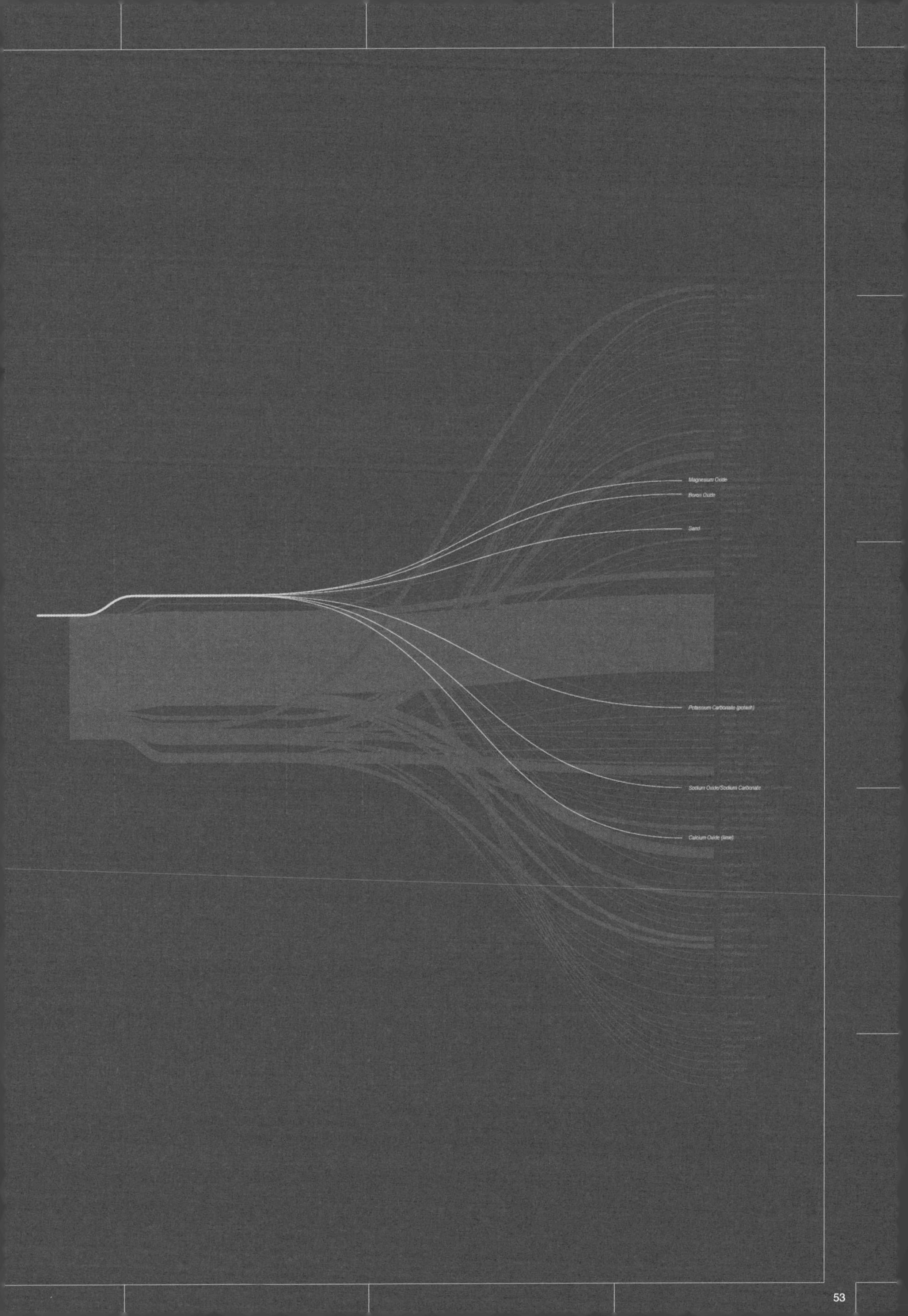
Magnesium Oxide
Boron Oxide
Sand
Potassium Carbonate (potash)
Sodium Oxide/Sodium Carbonate
Calcium Oxide (lime)

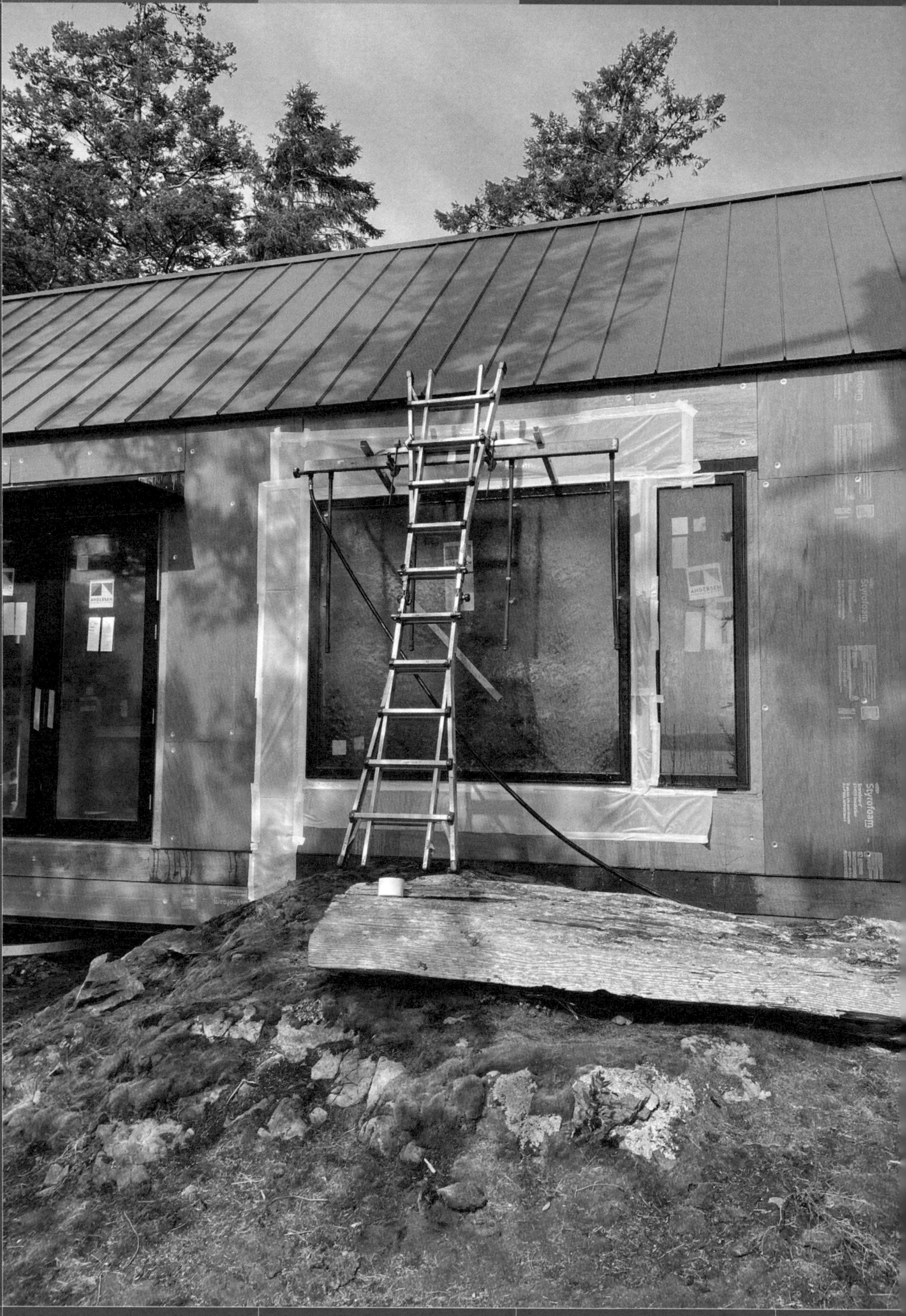
ANDERSEN
Styrofoam
Styrofoam

Glass in the house

1.5 tons of glass in house

\+ *Air and water pressure testing for windows, in a photo by Vikramaditya Prakash.*

Industrial Sand

Roughly 70% of glass—by mass—is sand, or more specifically silicon dioxide. Unlike the sand used in mixtures of concrete or asphalt paving, the sand required for flat glass needs to be more than 95% pure silicon dioxide and ideally consists of grains that are uniform in size, between 0.075 mm and 1.18 mm in diameter. This particular category of sand is generally referred to as "industrial sand."

The industrial sand used for glass must be of sufficient purity and of specific morphologies. The sand must contain only around 0.1% of iron oxide by mass, as any more would produce a greenish tint in the final product. For glass of higher optical specification than common pane glass, the iron content must be a tenth or even a hundredth less than this. Other metallic oxides in the sand might also produce other colored tints in the glass, and as such, even with purer sand, it is usually chemically washed before glass manufacture.

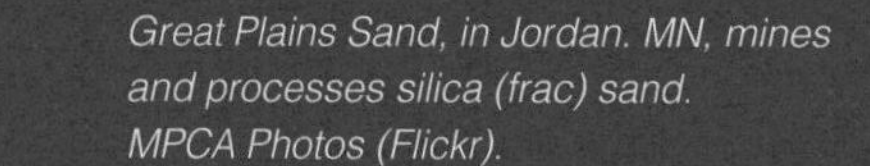

+ *Great Plains Sand, in Jordan. MN, mines and processes silica (frac) sand. MPCA Photos (Flickr).*

Fluxes

In general, fluxes are added to ceramic, glass, and metal production to lower the ingredients' melting points. Soda, potash, lithia, and boric oxide are some of the common fluxes used in glass production to bring the melting point of the glass batch down from around 1700°C to a much more workable 800–1000°C. For soda-lime glass, which includes most construction glass, the main fluxes are soda (sodium carbonate) and potash (potassium oxide).

Soda Ash and the Solvay Process

Soda, from the Arabic "suwwad", is also known as soda ash or sodium carbonate. It has been used in manufacturing for over 5,000 years. Pharonic Egyptians dug it up from dry lake beds to make glass ornaments and vessels. Today, the white, powdery substance is also used in the treatment of water, but also in everyday household baking soda.

Soda is typically industrially produced in the Solvay process with the reaction of concentrated brine and ammonia, although the discovery of trona in the mid-20th century has provided a naturally occurring mineral from which to process sodium carbonate. Prior to the Solvay process (and the preceding LeBlanc process), soda was primarily produced from the boiling of ash from specific land plants or seaweed. In other words, industrial glass as we know it today would not be possible without the quantities of sodium carbonate that can be produced with the Solvay process.

+ *A production site for sodium carbonate near Dombasle-sur-Meurthe, France, in a photo by Jeroen Komen (Wikimedia Commons).*

+ *Sodium carbonate in a photo by ChemicalInterest (Wikimedia Commons).*

+ *The Solvay Process Company, SHT Building, Solvay, Onondaga County, NY, in a Historic American Buildings Survey (HAER NY,34-SOLV,1H-1) photo (Wikimedia Commons).*

Colorado Plateau
evaporation ponds
potash mine

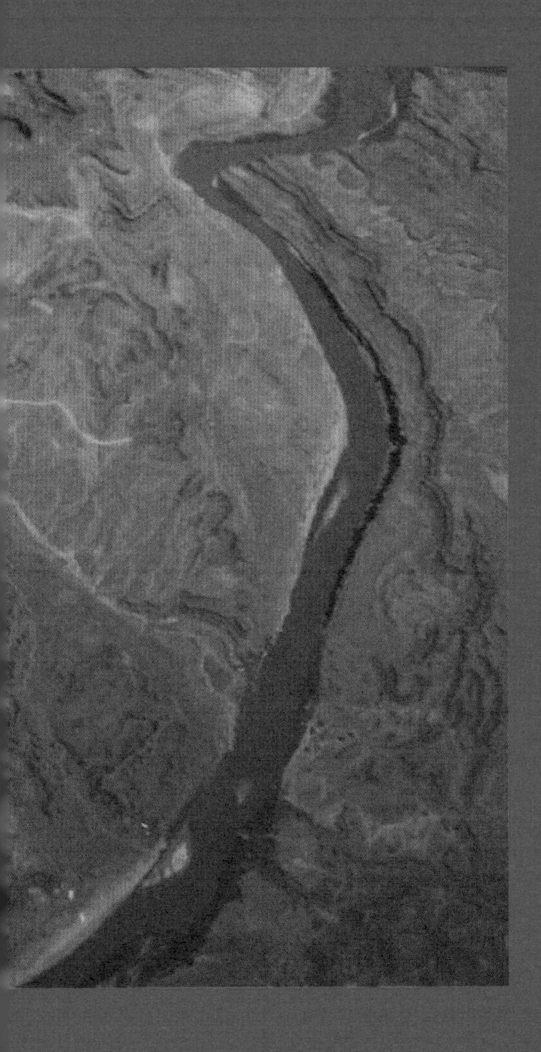

Potash and Structural Glass

One flux commonly used in the production of glass is potash, a term that refers to several potassium compounds, though it is usually potassium carbonate that is added to glass mixtures. Its addition can also be used to strengthen glass. Chemically strengthened glass is heated to specific temperatures to encourage ion exchange, without losing its molecular structure. When larger potassium ions replace the smaller sodium ions, compressive stress on the glass structure increases its strength.

\+ *Potash evaporation ponds near Moab, UT, in a photo by Doc Searls (Wikimedia Commons).*

\+ *Potash mine and evaporation ponds near Moab, UT, in a photo by NASA (Wikimedia Commons).*

\+ *A worker sampling Potash minerals in Saskatchewan, Canada, in a photo by Georgialh (Wikimedia Commons).*

Stabilizers

In addition to fluxes, stabilizers are added to the glass batch in order to adjust its viscosity, physical hardness, and chemical resistance. The first pieces of man-made glass likely came about as a by-product of ceramics, a process which also made use of calcium carbonate in the form of ground limestone. Whilst most construction glass is soda-lime glass, there are more specialized types of glass.

Lime is the most common of stabilizers and has been in use for glass production as far back as 3500 BCE. Limestone and dolomite are the most common sources of lime, which when melted into the glass batch release carbon dioxide and leave calcium oxide in the glass.

Magnesium Oxide

Often added together with lime in the form of dolomite, magnesium oxide is yet another common stabilizer that performs a similar function to lime, with the added benefit of increasing thermal stability and melt viscosity.

+ *Right: Magnesium oxide storage in a photo by DOE Photo (Wikimedia Commons). Magnesium oxide in a photo by Adam Redzikowski (Wikimedia Commons).*

+ *Below: Scanning electron microscopy and sample of Calcium oxide power (Wikipedia Commons).*

81
81
80

Lead Oxide

Lead oxide is another compound commonly added to glass, although in carefully controlled amounts. The compound can increase glass's chemical resistance, but too much lead lowers the melting temperature and decreases its hardness. Historically, lead oxide has seen more significant use in glass for decorative purposes, and in tableware.

Boron Oxide

Although primarily used in the production of optical glass, boron oxide is another stabilizer that is often added to the basic glass batch. As the number of borate producers in the United States is limited, most of the trade data related to borates is withheld to prevent loss of proprietary data. We do know, however, that most of the borate products in the United States are manufactured locally, and the two largest producers are located in Southern California.

+ *Lead powder burning in a photo by ChemicalInterest (Wikimedia Commons).*

+ *Boron trioxide powder in a photo by Materialscientist (Wikimedia Commons).*

Aluminum Oxide (Alumina)

Aluminum oxide is a stabilizer that adjusts the chemical properties of glass. When added to the batch, the aluminum oxide groupings essentially fill in the gaps in the silicon crystalline structure, leading to better chemical resistance while also increasing the viscosity of the glass at lower temperatures.

+ *Making alumina from clay, as seen in a photo from the National Institute of Standards and Technology (Wikimedia Commons).*

+ *Aluminum oxide powder in a photo by Aariuser I (Wikimedia Commons).*

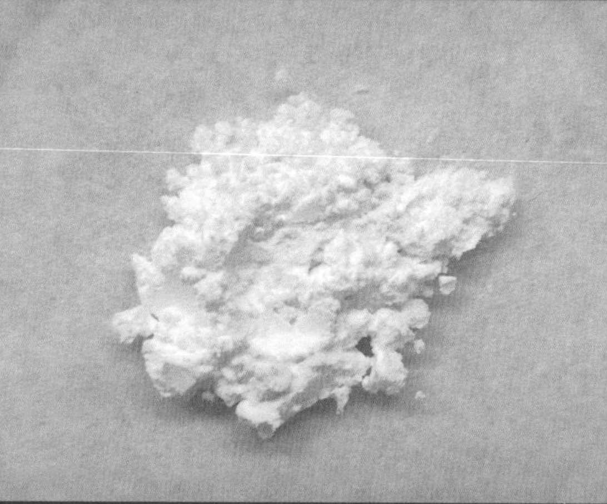

Plastics

+ *HDPE pipe installation in a photo by Tomascastelazo (Wikimedia Commons).*

The United States produces about 234 lbs (106.2 kg) of plastic waste per person, per year. (One barrel of oil weighs approximately 275 lbs.) Today, petrochemical plastics are omnipresent in buildings. The construction sector, the second largest consumer of plastics behind packaging, accounts for 16% of plastic's total global consumption.

Plastic are extremely durable materials that can be industrially produced cheaply and easily. While the production of plastics releases carbon diaoxide trapped in long buried fossils, plastic's durability raises questions about it best, limited use. The highest use of plastics is in packaging, a short-term single time use that is unquestionably a problem. Its limited deployment in the construction industry could be more justified, given the longevity of its use.

Plastics are typically deployed skeuomorphically, i.e. to replace products made from other materials. For example, vinyl siding and vinyl window frames are designed to replace wood construction; composite plastic roof tiles mimic and function as slate shingles.

In the Seattle house, the plastic tubing and pipping are an alternative to copper piping. Where as the PVDF resin coating enables the exterior sheet metal to last longer, the polyurethane foam insulation insulates the foam efficiently.

Many types of synthetic plastic polymers can be found in the house, including:

- 218 cubic feet of building insulation (polyurethane)

- 20 feet of ABS piping (Acrylonitrile-Butadiene-Styrene)

- 100 feet of PEX tubing (cross-linked polyethylene)

- 1000 square feet of PVDF resin coating (fluoropolymer).

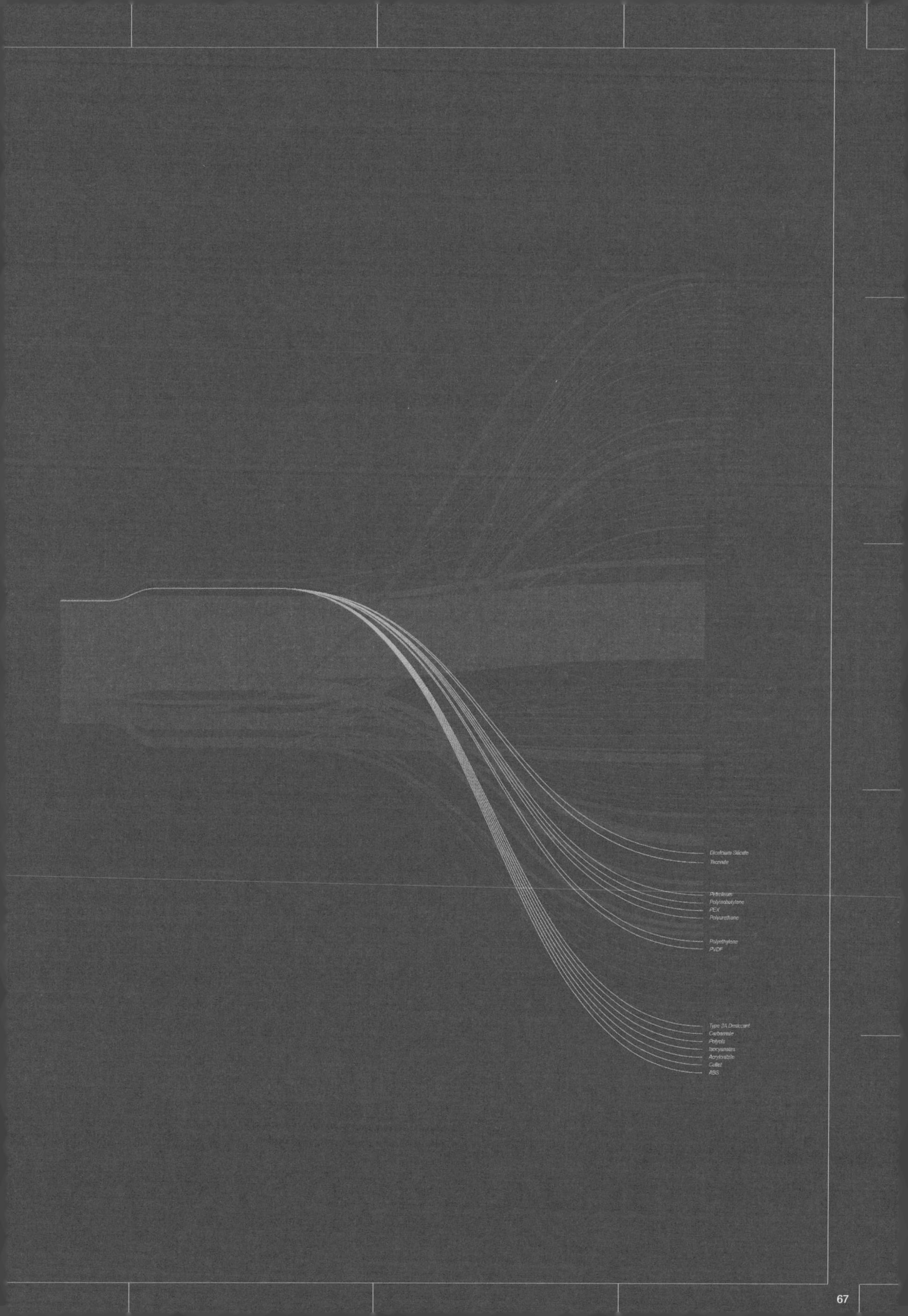
Dicalcium Silicate
Taconite
Petroleum
Polyisobutylene
PEX
Polyurethane
Polyethylene
PVDF
Type 3A Desiccant
Carbamide
Polyols
Isocyanates
Acrylonitrile
Cullet
ABS

"Do I recycle? Yes. Do I think it is a solution to plastic? Hell no. ...So recycling is good for ethics, you can be a good citizen. It's better than nothing, but it is not the solution, because it actually allows the problem to continue—it allows that tap to keep going, that bathtub tap to keep going. It gives ya some mops.

Dr. MAX LIBOIRON on Reorienting Within a World of Plastic, For the Wild Podcast hosted by Ayana Young.

Just five kinds of plastic constitute over 90% of all plastic produced (by weight):

(34.4%) **polyethylene** = LDC pipes, HDPE pipes

+ *Left: HDPE groundwater pipe installation in a photo by Energy.gov (Wikimedia Commons).*

(24.2%) **polypropylene** = ropes, addative

+ *Below: Polypropylene rope and textiles in photos by Peterlewis (Wikimedia Commons) and TextileMuseum Tilburg (Wikimedia Commons).*

(16.5%) **polyvinyl chloride** = PVC pipes+

+ *Below: PVC pipes in photographs by Srahman (Wikimedia Commons) and Steve Tan (Wikimedia Commons).*

(7.7%) **polyethylene terephthalate** = packaging

(7.3%) **polystyrene** = packaging

+ *Right: Polystyrene packaging in a photo by Acdx (Wikimedia Commons).*

"If I run a design class, I would fail the students who turned in the temporary use with the longest-lived material combination sort of design idea."

Plastic Packaging and the Plastisphere

“Plastics, whether they're wasteful or not, are an inextricable part of living systems. Everything from the fillings in your teeth to your contraceptive devices, to parts of your bones… they're part about making our infrastructures work, they're in highways and airplanes, and they make automobiles safe, they're in pacemakers… So, they're already inextricable parts of systems.

But then a few years ago, scientists found that when plastics enter certain types of ecosystems, mostly marine ones, they grow unique one-of-a-kind little tiny ecosystems on them. So, the bacteria and the sort of organisms that eat the bacterium and go around it don't grow in the same combinations anywhere else, and that they chose to call the plastisphere: the unique ecosystems that only exist with plastics. This is what makes plastics particularly interesting as a pollutant…

[But] I'm not saying, “Yay plastic, let's plastic it up, ...” but there are certain things that plastic is good at, and that we need it for, and certain things that shouldn't be used for, like packaging. Packaging can get used for a few minutes, and ...you've used one of the most durable materials in the world, to do it. If I run a design class, I would fail the students who turned in the temporary use with the longest-lived material combination sort of design idea. So when people talk about the ubiquity of plastics, they usually mean disposables, or single-use…So, if you want to talk about the annihilation of packaging, that's very, very, very different than talking about the annihilation of plastics. That's the plastisphere part.

Dr. Max Liboiron on Reorienting Within a World of Plastic,
in “For the Wild” Podcast hosted by Ayana Young

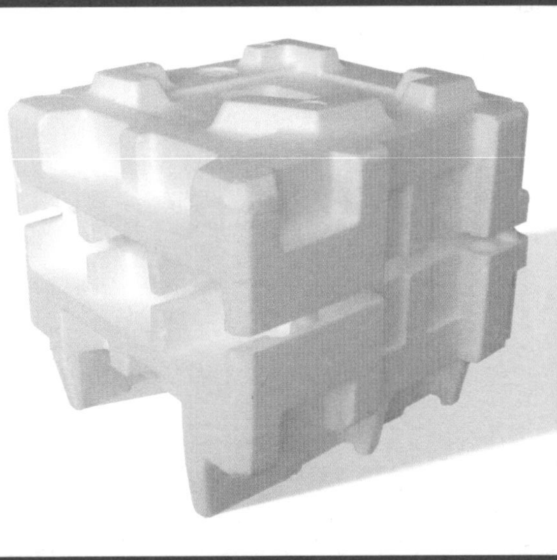

Polyurethane Foam Insulation

Dr. Otto Bayer (1902–82) is recognized as the “father” of the polyurethanes industry for his invention of the basic diisocyanate polyaddition process. The origin of polyurethane dates back to the beginning of WWII, when it was first developed as a replacement for rubber. By the end of the war, polyurethane coatings were being manufactured and used on an industrial scale and could be custom formulated for specific applications.

Polyurethanes were widely promoted after WWII as a resilient material that could be easily formed to suited disparate purposes.

Plastics in the house

218 cubic feet of polyurethane insulation

+ *Left: Otto Bayer in 1952 in a photo by Bayer AG (Wikimedia Commons).*

+ *Below: The installation of polyurethane insulation in a photo by Chicagosprayfoam (Wikimedia Commons).*

+ *The creation of polurethane foam in a photo by Christof Jelich (Wikimedia Commons).*

Steel

The United States consumes approximately 110 million tons of steel each year, with more than 40 million tons of it used in the construction industry.

The house contains 76.66 tons of steel in the structure, 0.58 tons of steel in the siding, and 9 tons in the steel staircase. As seen in the graphic at right, iron ore makes up the majority of steel's ingredients (by volume).

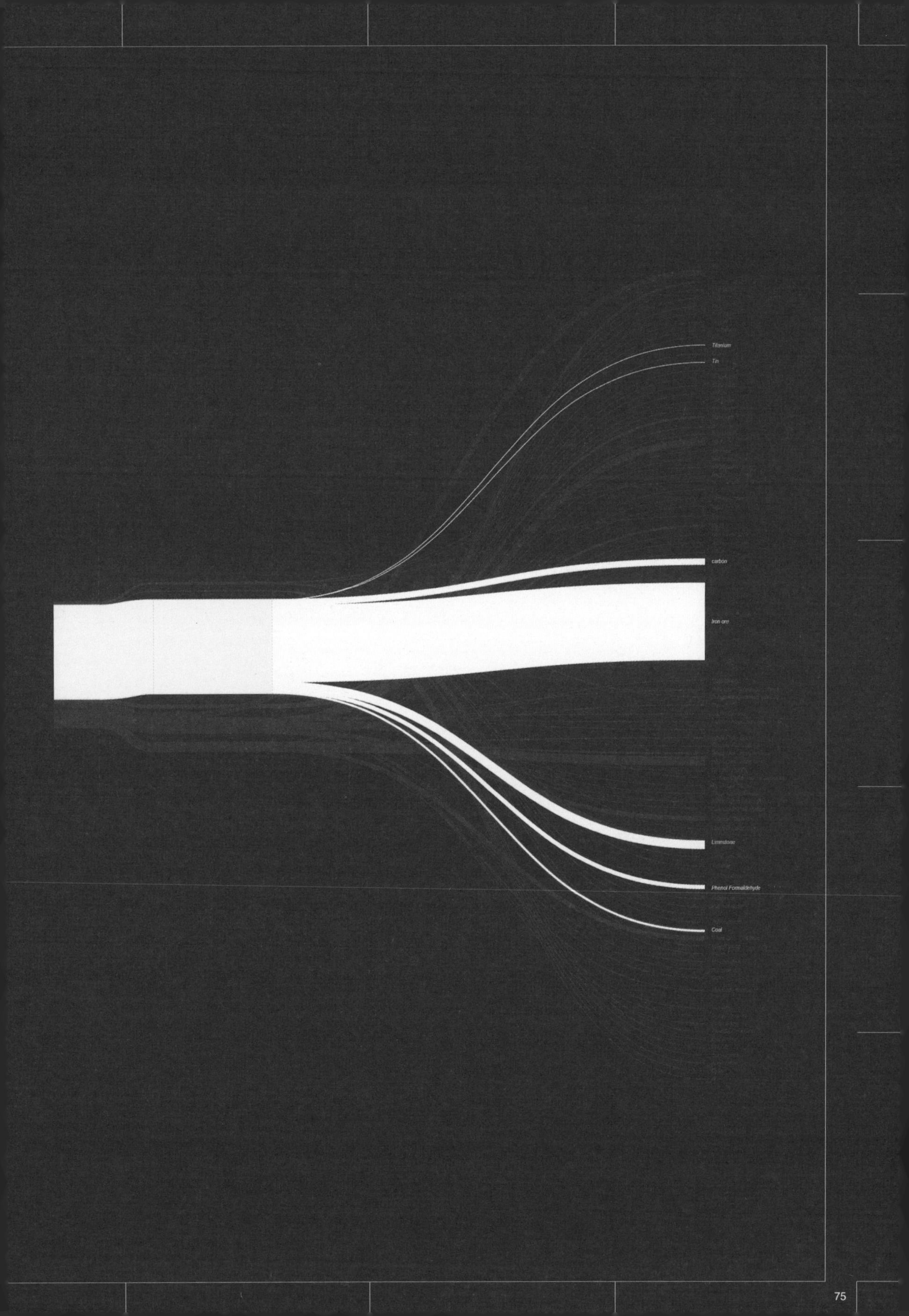
Titanium
Tin
carbon
Iron ore
Limestone
Phenol Formaldehyde
Coal

Structural Steel

The structural steel used in the house was sourced from Bear Creek Metal in Bothell, WA. Different steel members were produced at Steel Dynamics in Indiana, Bayou Steel Group in Tennessee, and Tung Ho Steel Enterprise Corporation in Kaohsiung City, Taiwan.

+ *A photo of the house under construction by Vikramaditya Prakash.*

Steel in house

76.66 tons of structural steel

Steel Siding

The house siding was sourced from D4 Systems LLC in Washington, who was supplied by AEP Span. AEP Span is owned by Bluescope, which is headquartered in Australia.

The steel coil siding is from Australia was then shipped to either Kalama, WA, or to Rancho Cucamonga, CA.

It is made of 25% post-consumer recycled content mixed with other iron ore in Port Kembla, Australia. There are no steel mills on the American West Coast that produce the type of steel used for metal roof and siding products.

+ *A photo of the house by Vikramaditya Prakash.*

Steel in the house

0.58 tons of steel siding

Steel Stair

The steel for the staircase was sourced from Nucor in Plymouth, UT, and Searing Industries in Rancho Cucamonga, CA. Nucor is the largest steel producer in the United States, and produced the steel sheets. Searing Industries provided the smaller steel connection parts that were produced in Korea and Taiwan.

+ *A photo of the house by Vikramaditya Prakash.*

9 tons of steel in the staircase

Ceramics

The list of chemical compounds that constitutes "ceramic" is quite similar to that of Portland cement, although the ratios of each ingredient vary significantly. Ceramic material is composed primarily of silicon dioxide from clay (66%), with smaller amounts of calcium oxide (lime) and aluminum oxide, as well as under 4% each of iron oxide, magnesium oxide, and potassium oxide.

Ceremics are an ancient construction material used, for instance, in the Indus Valley civilization about 3000 years ago. Today, ceramics are mainly used in the bathroom tiles and sanitary ware in residential construction, although ceramics are also available as an exterior cladding material.

While ceramics make for a durable material, they are prone to cracking (not as much of a problem with porcelain) and are much heavier than other cladding materials.

Overall, ceramics are considered to be environmentally friendly.

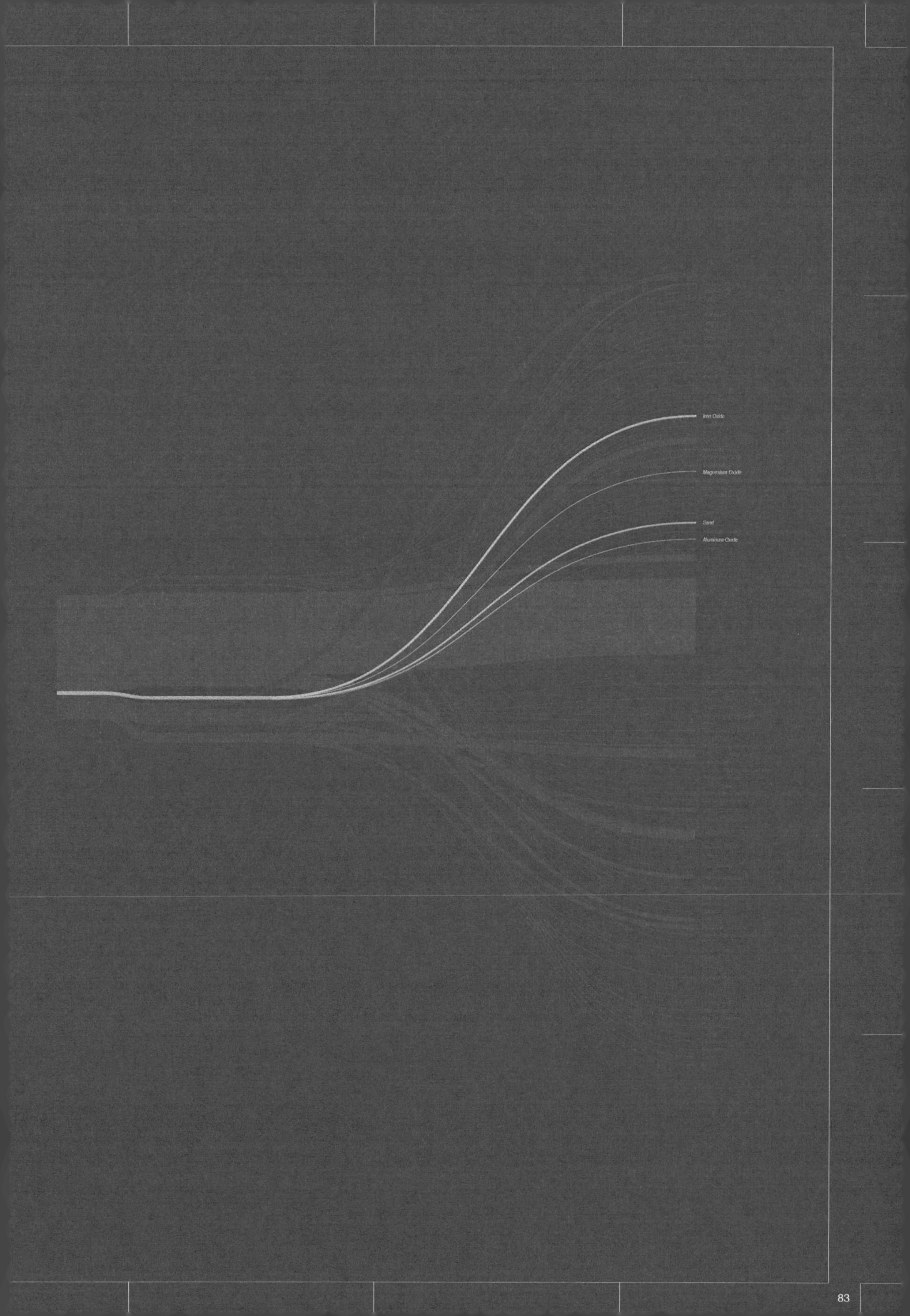
Iron Oxide
Magnesium Oxide
Sand
Aluminum Oxide

Drywall

Sheetrock, or drywall (as it is more generally known), is gypsum-based paneling often used to face interior walls and ceilings. While the exact quantity of drywall used in the Seattle house is unknown, it can be reasonably assumed that drywall covers every interior surface, given that the house employs wood-frame construction.

Upon extraction, raw gypsum (hydrous calcium sulfate) is transported to a manufacturing facility and combined with starch, paper pulp, thickening agents, and water. Other additives, such as accelerators, retarders, and agents to increase fire resistance, are added at this stage as well. The mixture is then blended to create a plaster-like substance, and sandwiched between two sheets of stiff paper. It is then dried in a heated drying chamber until stiff enough to use as a construction material.

Drywall constitutes about 15% of all construction and demolition debris in the United States. In landfills, overtime this can leach toxic chemicals into the surrounding land and groundwater. When decomposed anaerobically it releases hydrogen sulphide, which is poisonous to humans.

Drywall being produced and installed in photographs by Andrew Ryan Smith (Wikimedia Commons), Sally Mendzela (Wikimedia Commons), and ВОЛМА (Wikimedia Commons).

Concrete

An estimated 52.3 tons of concrete were used in the Seattle house, primarily in the ground floor slab, connections to the adjacent house, and structural systems such as the foundation and retaining walls.

The concrete was a mix composed of:
- 42% Portland cement
- 11% gravel
- 11% sand
- 14% fly ash
- 23% water
- MasterPolyheed 997, a water-reducing admixture
- Masterset AC 534, an accelerating admixture

Concrete has a long history as a construction material, being used to line underground cisterns in the desert 8,000 years ago. The Egyptians used it as a mortar, and the Romans built extensively with it, including, most famously, the Pantheon in Rome.

The first "proto" Portland cement was pioneered by bricklayer Joseph Aspdin in Leeds, England, in 1824, when he filed a patent for a mixture of synthesized limestone and clay, citing its resemblance to Portland stone. What began as an experimental venture laid the groundwork for nearly three decades of development around hydraulic, lime-based mixtures, culminating in a prototype of the Portland cement we know today by Isaac Charles Johnson in 1850.

Concrete enjoys a celebrated relationship with modern architecture, as for instance in its use in Fallingwater house by Frank LLoyd Wright (1939) and Le Corbusier's Unite d'Habitation towers in Europe.

After water, concrete is the most widely used material on earth. Worldwide, over ten billion tons of concrete are being produced each year. In the United States, about 370 million cubic yards of concrete are produced per year, with nearly 40% of it going into commercial real estate. That equals just over one cubic yard per person in the United States per year.

It is estimated that between 4-8% of the total global carbon dioxide emissions are retracable to concrete. Most of this is indexable to the production of cement.

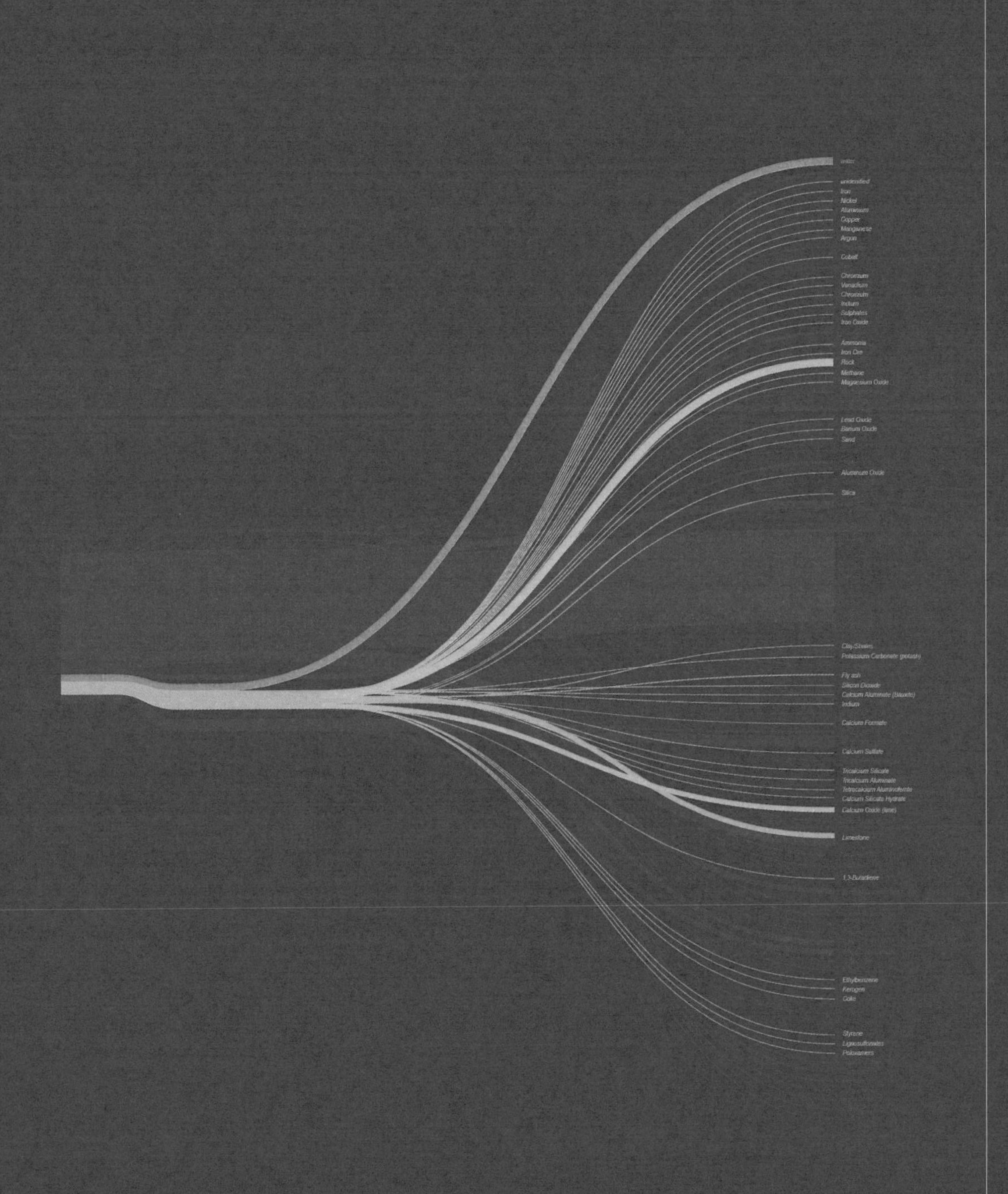
Iron
Nickel
Aluminium
Copper
Manganese
Argon
Cobalt
Chromium
Vanadium
Chromium
Indium
Sulphates
Iron Oxide
Ammonia
Iron Ore
Rock
Methane
Magnesium Oxide
Lead Oxide
Barium Oxide
Sand
Aluminum Oxide
Silica
Clay/Shales
Potassium Carbonate (potash)
Fly ash
Silicon Dioxide
Calcium Aluminate (Bauxite)
Indium
Calcium Formate
Calcium Sulfate
Tricalcium Silicate
Tricalcium Aluminate
Tetracalcium Aluminoferrite
Calcium Silicate Hydrate
Calcium Oxide (lime)
Limestone
1,3-Butadiene
Ethylbenzene
Kerogen
Coke
Styrene
Lignosulfonates
Poloxamers

Portland Cement

Portland cement is composed of:
- lime
- clay
- silica
- aluminum oxide
- iron oxide
- magnesium oxide

In order to produce portland cement, limestone and clay are quarried. In the case of the Seattle house, this occurred at the Lafarge Quarry and the Sumas Mountain, respectively. The raw materials are then crushed to pieces that are 3 inches or less in diameter, and ground with other ingredients such as iron ore, silica fume, and aluminum oxide. All of this is fed into a kiln, which heats the finely ground material to 2700˚F (1482˚C). While some compounds, such as carbon dioxide, are driven off in the form of gases during the heating process, the remaining materials form a new substance called clinker. Once the clinker has cooled, it is ground even further, and small amounts of gypsum are added to control the hardening rate of the final cementitious product. At the end of the manufacturing process, cement particles have an average diameter of 15 microns.

Portland cement is classified as hydraulic, meaning that it hardens through a chemical reaction with water, or through hydration. During hydration, a node forms on the surface of each cement particle. The node expands until it links with nodes from other cement particles, or adheres to pieces of aggregate. Approximately 842 kg of hot water was added to the concrete mix for the construction of the house.

While cement constitutes only about 10-15% of concrete's mass, it is responsible for over 90% of its greenhouse gas emissions. About 40% of emissions released by the production of cement come from the fossil fuels that are burnt to the heat the limestone to make clinker. However, the remaining 60% are a result of the carbon dioxide that is released when limestone or calcium carbonate is heated to break it down into carbon oxide. Most limestone was formed shallow marine conditions through a process of pressurized sedimination which is why it, like oil, has a high percentage of sequestered carbon.

Limestone decarbonization accounts for about 7% of the worlds carbon dioxide emissions.

Concrete in the house

52.3 tons of concrete

of which 42% (22 tons) is Portland cement

+ *A cement mix with a typical Portland cement texture in a photo by Denslenovo (Wikimedia Commons).*

Gypsum

The primary purpose of gypsum in Portland cement is to regulate its setting time. Gypsum acts as a retardant by reacting with the tricalcium aluminates present in cement to produce a colloidal gel, which prevents flash setting and allows for mixing, transportation, and pouring time.

Bauxite

There are various conventional sources for the iron oxide used in cement, including iron ore, scrap iron, and fly ash. The ferrous compound makes up 0.5% to 6% of Portland cement. Despite the small amount, iron oxide's role in cement is tripartite: not only does it increase the compressive strength of cement by reacting with aluminum and calcium to produce tricalcium aluminoferrite, it acts as a fluxing agent, which lowers the melting point of silica from 3000°F to 2600°F during the production of clinker nodules that are eventually ground to make the cement. Various types of iron oxide can also be used to pigment cement.

Bauxite is sedimentary rock with a high percentage of aluminum. It is usually strip-mined because most of it occurs at or near the surface of the earth.

Concrete in the house

52.3 tons of concrete

of which 42% (22 tons) is Portland cement

+ *A bauxite mine in central Jamaica in a photo by Paul Morris (Wikimedia Commons).*

Aggregate

The convention of adding large amounts of aggregate to an otherwise cementitious mix to produce concrete can be attributed to ancient Roman technologies. In contrast to today's concrete, however, which specifically requires the use of inert, non-reactive substances as aggregate, Roman concrete used volcanic rock, which contained pozzolanic compounds, instead. The volcanic rock reacted with compounds in the cement, increasing the concrete's strength over time. Furthermore, Roman concrete employed seawater as its liquid component, rather than freshwater—another difference from today's concrete industry conventions, where seawater is avoided at all costs due to the risk of chloride and sulfur erosion. It has been found that seawater reacted with the volcanic ash in Roman cement, and induced the formation of new minerals, such as Al-tobermorite and phillipsite, which actually increased the concrete's resistance to fracture.

The aggregate used in concrete today is composed primarily of gravel and sand. The latter is most commonly dredged from riverbeds or, in the case of the Seattle house, dug from an open-pit sandstone mine. Upon extraction, the sandstone is crushed, filtered through perforated screens to separate different sized particles, washed of silt and clay residue, and—in some cases—crushed further to obtain specific morphologies. Though inert, properties of the chosen aggregate (such as moisture content, abrasiveness/texture, and size) significantly impact the workability and compressive strength of the final concrete mixture.

Concrete in the house

52.3 tonnes of concrete:

11% (5.8 tons) gravel
11% (5.8 tons) sand

+ *Aggregate piles in Fort Loudon, TN, in a Library of Congress (LC-DIG-fsac-1a35246) photo (Wikimedia Commons).*

Fly Ash

Fly ash is an industrial byproduct of coal-fired electricity (and steam)generating plants. It is classified, along with bottom ash, boiler slag, and gypsum, as a Coal Combustion Product (CCP) by the American Coal Ash Association. During the combustion process, impurities present in the pulverized coal produce a molten mineral residue. This residue hardens to form two types of coal ash particulates, differentiated based on particle size: bottom ash, which settles at the base of the power plant's boiler, and fly ash, which is airborne, and rises into the plant's exhaust stacks. The addition of fly ash to the cement mixture serves a similar purpose to that of silica fume—as a pozzolan rich in siliceous and aluminum compounds, it reacts chemically with calcium hydroxide in the presence of water to form compounds possessing cementitious properties.

The lightweight nature of fly ash particulates makes them highly conducive to becoming air pollutants, and requires fly ash to be disposed of in a specific manner. Coal ash containment ponds are a type of landfill used to prevent coal ash from polluting the air. The ash is mixed with water to minimize its release into the atmosphere.

The United States currently has 1400 ash dumps—a combination of landfills and ponds—all over the country. Several disastrous ash spills have occurred as a result of this disposal method, such as the 2014 spill into the Dan River from the Eden, NC, Duke Energy facility. During the event, 39,000 tons of coal ash and 27 million gallons of wastewater were released into the river due to a burst drainage pipe at the plant's containment pond.

Concrete in the house

52.3 tons of concrete:

14% (7.3 tons) fly ash

+ *A fly ash pile seen in a photo by the US Department of Energy (Wikimedia Commons).*

Admixtures

One of the defining characteristics of 21st-century concrete is the prevalent use of additives, or admixtures, used to alter its chemical properties. There are five distinct categories of admixture: air-entraining, water-reducing, retarding, accelerating, and plasticizing. The presence of chemical additives has allowed for the use of secondary industrial materials in cementitious mixtures (such as slag and fly ash), thus reducing the need for virgin material extraction.

Several admixtures, sourced from BASF, were added to the concrete used for the house. MasterPolyheed 997 was used to reduce the water needed in the mix, which also increased the post-hydration strength of the concrete. Masterset AC 534 was used to accelerate its set time.

Water-reducing admixtures, as the name suggests, decrease the amount of water required for a concrete mixture to achieve a certain slump, usually by 5–10%. Because less water is used during the mixing stage, the cement-water ratio is increased, and the hardened concrete has comparatively higher compressive strength.

Accelerators decrease the setting time of concrete, and thus increase the rate of its strength development. While this may seem counterintuitive, accelerators are often used when concrete is being poured in cold weather, when environmental factors could potentially freeze the concrete before it properly sets. This is likely why an accelerating admixture was used in the construction of the Seattle house.

Concrete in the house

52.3 tons of concrete:

MasterPolyheed 997, a water-reducing admixture
Masterset AC 534, an accelerating admixture

Wood

Wood is a primary ingredient of the Seattle house. It made its way into the building in three forms, lumber in the house structure, plywood in its partitions, and aggregated in its parquet flooring.

The structural lumber and plywood are mainly Douglas fir pine, coming from within the state of Washington, while the parquet's white oak was sourced from Germany before being processed in Indonesia.

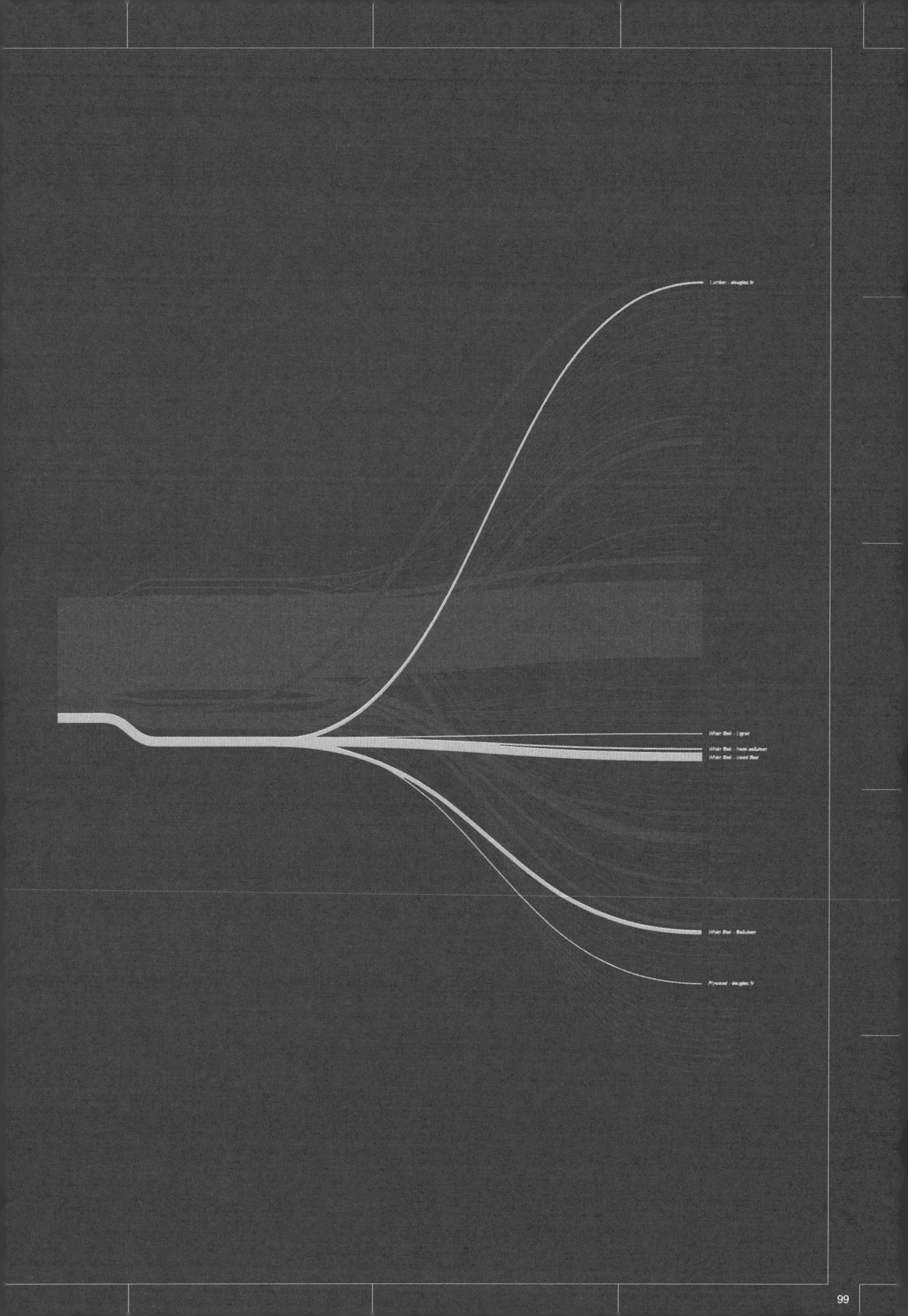
Lumber - douglas fir
White Oak - Lignin
White Oak - hemi-cellulose
White Oak - wood fiber
White Oak - Cellulose
Plywood - douglas fir

Framing

The platform-framing method used in the Seattle house descended from its older sister, the balloon-framing method, which was first introduced in the 1830s in the region of Chicago, IL. The latter requires a large number of thin wood elements, generally standard 2x4 lumber, but promises a straightforward assembly process. This method boomed in areas rich in softwood forests—such as the United States and Canada—that lacked the critical mass of skilled builders needed to house its new settlers.

Once widespread—when long lumber was plentiful—balloon framing has been largely replaced by platform framing. Based on the same principle of "studs" nailed together to form a sturdy, light skeleton, platform framing requires shorter elements. In it, each stud only runs from the sill plate to the top plate, rather than the full height of the building. Though nailed to those above and below, each story is largely structurally independent.

+ *A photo of the house under construction by Vikramaditya Prakash.*

ENVISION
DO NOT DROP ON END
ENVISION

Flooring

Parquet is derived from the French term "parquetry," meaning "small pieces, small compartment." Timber contrasting in color and grain, such as oak, walnut, cherry, and maple, are often employed to enhance the designs.

Parquet floors were first developed in France in the 1600s as an alternative to the expensive and hard to maintain marble flooring. Stone finished floors required recurrent water treatment that tended to rot the underlying wood framework joins.

Parquet became the epitome of elegance in institutions buildings and manor houses in the 1680s when Louis XIV installed exceptional parquet designs in his Versailles palace. This act sparked a trend in Europe and beyond; for centuries onwards, parquet—representing excellent and careful craftsmanship—remained a symbol of luxury and opulence.

With the garment boom of the 1930s, however, and subsequent industrialization of carpet flooring, parquet fell out of vogue and went into sharp decline. Many were covered-up, hidden, and forgotten, until the end of the last century when fashions changed and a plethora of parquet floors was unveiled and restored.

Historically, parquet floors consisted of pieces of plain wood that were installed on concrete or hot bitumen and then hand-leveled by artisans on-site. Improvements in wood product manufacturing and discoveries in resins and polymer adhesive allowed for greater standardization of the wood pieces and more efficient assembling techniques. As labor cost increased in the West, such pre-manufactured pieces allowed for a sharp reduction in on-site work. Nowadays, due to the explosion of parquet demand, the rarity of precious hardwoods, and to prevent further deforestation, it is rare to find parquet floors assembled from plain, solid wood elements. Instead, as it is the case in the house in Seattle, the top—white oak—layer represents only 10% of the parquet thickness. The rest is a filling composed of crushed wood coming from fast-growing trees such as Sengon or Rubberwood.

The white oak used for the surface of the flooring was sourced in Germany, shipped to Indonesia where the filling wood is grown, the parquet manufactured, and then shipped to the United States for installation.

+ *Wood flooring from the house in a photo by Vikramaditya Prakash.*

Plywood

Plywood is a material manufactured from thin layers, or "plies," of wood that are glued together with adjacent layers having their grain rotated up to 90 degrees to one another. Such an assembly process makes plywood stiff enough to replace plain wood sheets that are sturdier but harder to source.

Every year, the United States produces roughly 750 million cubic feet of plywood. Stacked to a height of one foot, such a quantity equals 27 square miles—the footprint of a small city.

If plywood can be made from hardwoods, softwoods, or a combination of the two, in the United States, it is most commonly assembled from Douglas fir. Such softwood trees, growing mostly in the Western part of the continent, from Canada to the Mountain of Mexico, are by far the most common species in the USA by volume: accounting for 12.8% of the total volume (2002), nearly twice as much as any other species. A significant reason is the Douglas fir rapid growth, with full growth in 50 to 80 years, out producing most other species in North America.

While plywood is not biodegradable like wood, it is generally considered to very environmentally friendly because its production involves almost no emission of green house gases.

+ *A Malaysian plywood factory in a photo by CEphoto, Uwe Aranas (Wikimedia Commons).*

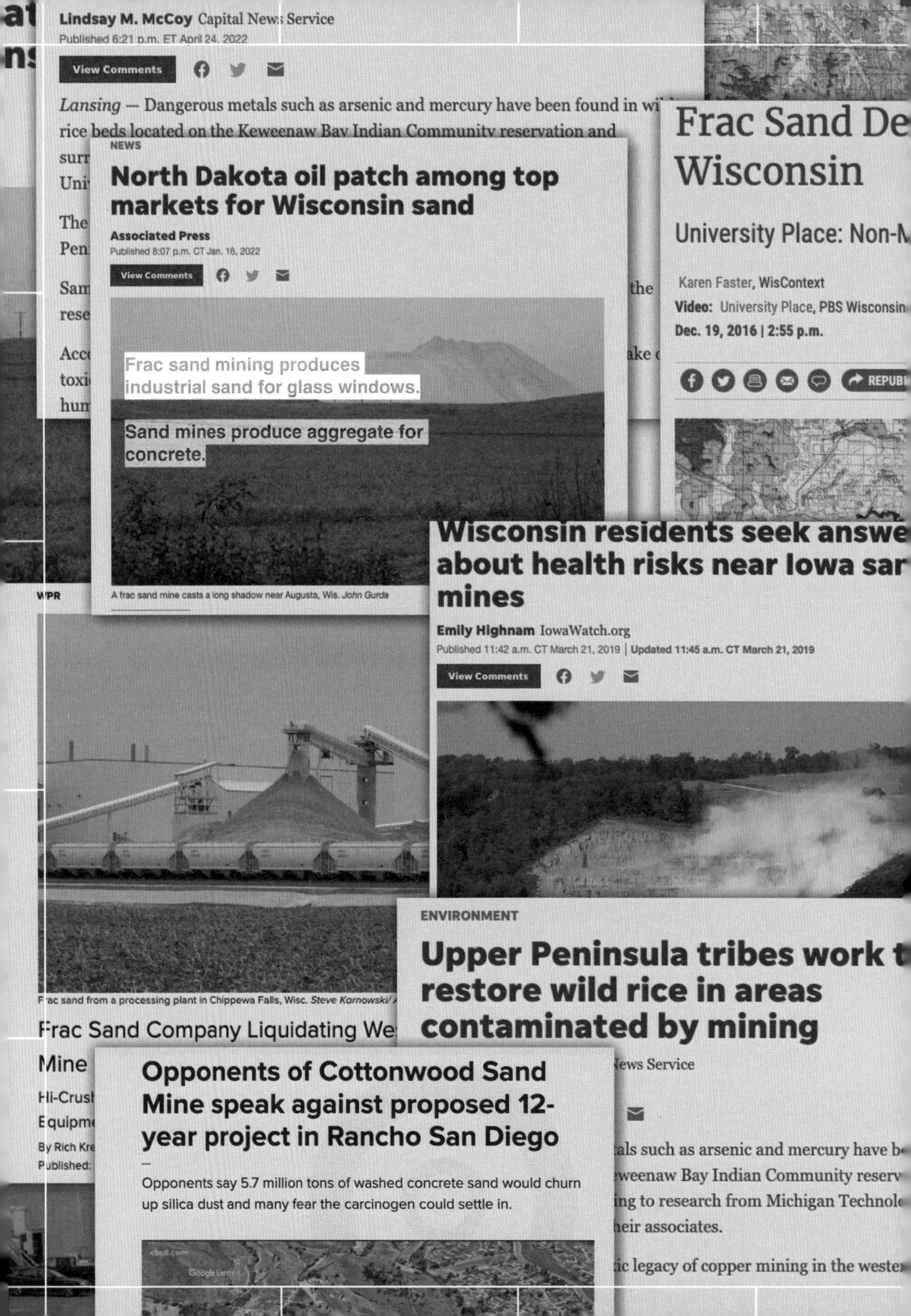

Lindsay M. McCoy Capital News Service
Published 6:21 p.m. ET April 24, 2022

View Comments

Lansing — Dangerous metals such as arsenic and mercury have been found in wi
rice beds located on the Keweenaw Bay Indian Community reservation and

NEWS

North Dakota oil patch among top markets for Wisconsin sand

Associated Press
Published 8:07 p.m. CT Jan. 16, 2022

View Comments

Frac sand mining produces industrial sand for glass windows.

Sand mines produce aggregate for concrete.

A frac sand mine casts a long shadow near Augusta, Wis. *John Gurda*

Frac Sand De
Wisconsin

University Place: Non-N

Karen Faster, WisContext
Video: University Place, PBS Wisconsin
Dec. 19, 2016 | 2:55 p.m.

REPUB

Wisconsin residents seek answe about health risks near Iowa sar mines

Emily Highnam IowaWatch.org
Published 11:42 a.m. CT March 21, 2019 | **Updated 11:45 a.m. CT March 21, 2019**

View Comments

WPR

Frac sand from a processing plant in Chippewa Falls, Wisc. *Steve Karnowski/*

Frac Sand Company Liquidating We
Mine

Hi-Crus
Equipm

By Rich Kre
Published:

ENVIRONMENT

Upper Peninsula tribes work t restore wild rice in areas contaminated by mining

ews Service

als such as arsenic and mercury have b
weenaw Bay Indian Community reserv
ing to research from Michigan Technol
heir associates.

ic legacy of copper mining in the weste

Opponents of Cottonwood Sand Mine speak against proposed 12-year project in Rancho San Diego

Opponents say 5.7 million tons of washed concrete sand would churn up silica dust and many fear the carcinogen could settle in.

cbs8.com
Google Earth

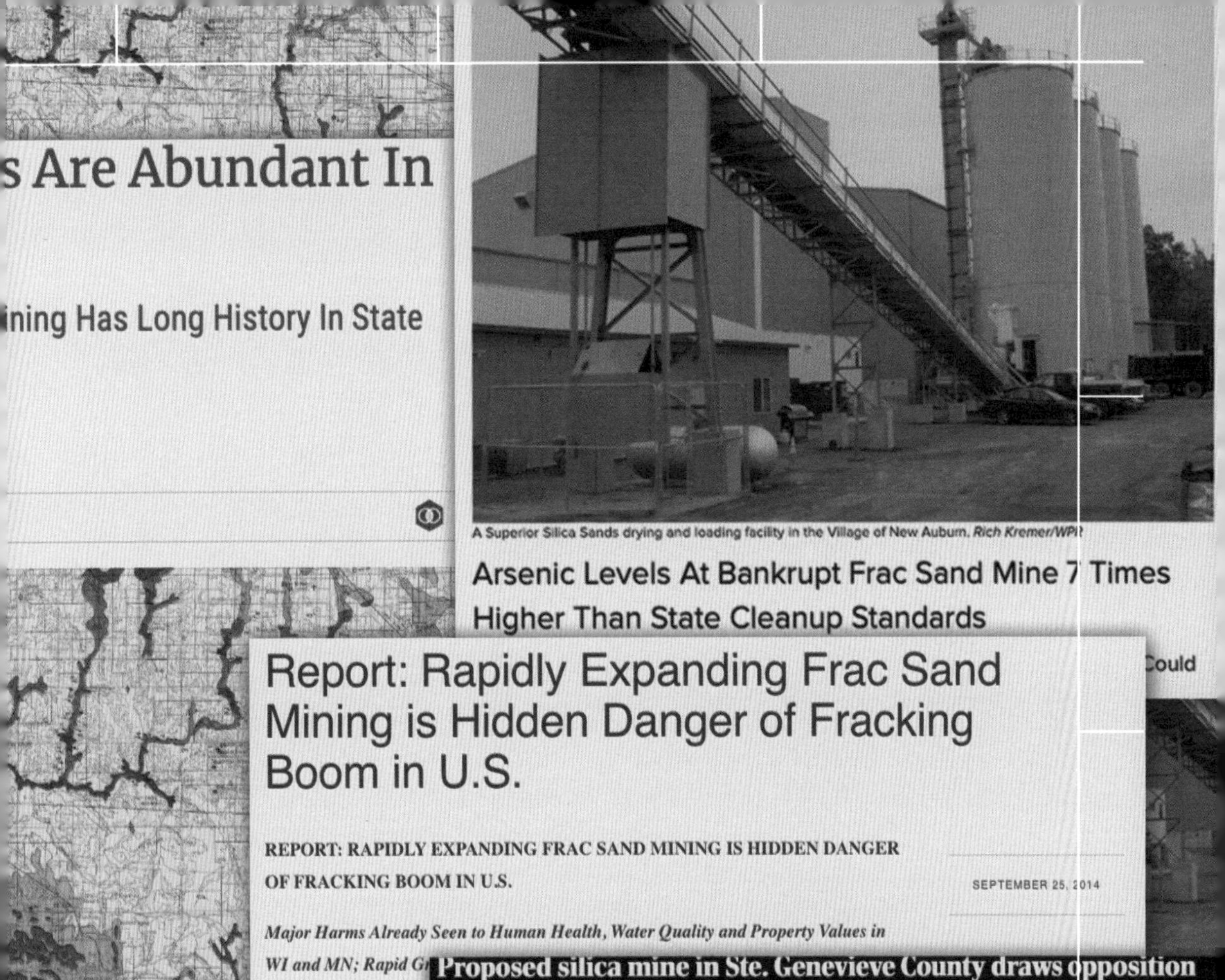
s Are Abundant In
ining Has Long History In State
A Superior Silica Sands drying and loading facility in the Village of New Auburn. Rich Kremer/WPR
Arsenic Levels At Bankrupt Frac Sand Mine 7 Times Higher Than State Cleanup Standards
Could
Report: Rapidly Expanding Frac Sand Mining is Hidden Danger of Fracking Boom in U.S.
REPORT: RAPIDLY EXPANDING FRAC SAND MINING IS HIDDEN DANGER OF FRACKING BOOM IN U.S.
SEPTEMBER 25, 2014
Major Harms Already Seen to Human Health, Water Quality and Property Values in WI and MN; Rapid Gr
MA, MI, MO, NY, NC
BOSTON, MA///Sept
particle sand needed fo
Proposed silica mine in Ste. Genevieve County draws opposition
Jack Suntrup Apr 18, 2022 0

to this article now
ered by Trinity Audio
1.0x
10:11
Wisconsin Tribe Halts $1.5 Billion Open-Pit Mine
To protect vital wetlands, the Ojibwe tribe and local scientists and activists pressured industry to abandon plans for what would have harmed thousands of species of plants and animals.
Protect
our
FARMS, COUNTY,
WATER

Potash is an ingredient in glass windows.
Fly ash is an ingredient in concrete.
Feds approve massive potash mine on dry Utah lakebed; it could bring hundreds of jobs, millions in sales
Courtesy photo by Peak Minerals The BLM has approved a 125,000-acre complex of evaporati
NEWS
What is New Mexico doing about Mosaic Potash's water pollution in Carlsbad?
Adrian Hedden
Carlsbad Current-Argus
Published 8:27 a.m. MT April 21, 2022 | Updated 10:30 a.m. MT April 22, 2022
View Comments
Carlsbad's potash mines are s
only deposits in the country.
Carlsbad Current-Argus

Gambling ... merica's Amazon'

›ama's largest utility plans to bury a
eap of toxic coal waste in one of
rth America's most biodiverse river
›ms. Experts say it wi...
ion's most pristine w...

'5.7 million metric tonnes of fly ash in Ennore backwaters, flood plains'

"New developments (built-up land) and fly ash depositions in the study location have significantly reduced the natural drainage, thereby altering the hydrology and ecosystem of the entire region."

11th April 2022 02:44 PM

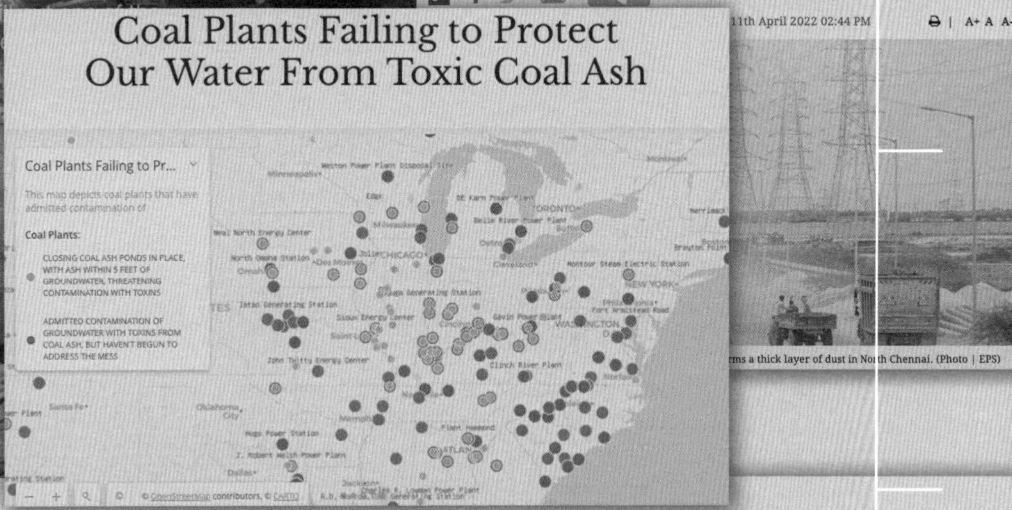

Coal Plants Failing to Protect
Our Water From Toxic Coal Ash
Coal Plants Failing to Pr...
This map depicts coal plants that have admitted contamination of
Coal Plants:
CLOSING COAL ASH PONDS IN PLACE, WITH ASH WITHIN 5 FEET OF GROUNDWATER, THREATENING CONTAMINATION WITH TOXINS
ADMITTED CONTAMINATION OF GROUNDWATER WITH TOXINS FROM COAL ASH, BUT HAVEN'T BEGUN TO ADDRESS THE MESS
CHICAGO
TORONTO
NEW YORK
WASHINGTON
© OpenStreetMap contributors, © CARTO

...rms a thick layer of dust in North Chennai. (Photo | EPS)

ENVIRONMENT

Biden administration takes action on toxic coal ash plaguing Kentucky and Indiana

Coal ash is produced primarily from th...

HOME > NEWS >

New Tests Can Detect Tiny but Toxic Particles of Coal Ash in Soil

Scientists at Duke University have developed a suite of four new tests that can be used to detect coal ash contamination in soil with unprecedented sensitivity.

July 22, 2021

What is the Future of Guinea's Mining Sector After the Coup?

Published in: Thomson Reuters Foundation

Jim Wormington

Bauxite is an essential ingredient in concrete.

Around 25% of the house's steel is made from scrap metal.

A woman in Lansanayah, a village 750 meters from a bauxite mine owned by La Société Minière de Boké consortium. © 2018

World

Red mud: Toxic waste of aluminun

CBC News · Posted: Oct 07, 2010 4:47 PM ET | Last Updated: October 7, 20

Red mud is a toxic byproduct of the industrial process that refines into aluminum oxide, or alumina.

(Alumina is put through a separate process, electrolysis, to make

Chinese outages a reminder of aluminum's secret: Andy Home

By Andy Home

7 MIN R

LONDON (Reuters) - Chinese alumina prices have jumped to a five on news that at least two refineries in the province of Shanxi are be pending environmental inspections.

TO: An ox is seen on mud after a tailings dam owned by Brazilian miner Vale SA burst, in Brumadinho,

An aerial view of the flooding at the Norsk Hydro Alunorte con riotimesonline.com found on Tw

The worst disaster, so far

What is likely the most serious accident yet, occurred in residents, major storms on February 16 and 17 caused an

Recycling what the world throws away
2 workers die after inhaling toxic gas at Ctg shipbreaking yard
Anwar Hussain, Chittagong
Published at 09:51 pm March 24th, 2020

Sources

Sources

Sources

Source consciousness— digging into the earth and chopping the forests

Materials for this house in Seattle were mined from all over the world. In some cases we were able to get specific information; but tracing all the sources is impossible, so we made the most informed guesses possible. There are two frames in the map at right: extraction and processing. Processing and finishing of the globally-sources materials took place in Europe, Africa, Asia, Australia, and the Americas. In some situations these extraction and processing sites are quite close. In others, they are far apart and have nothing connecting them apart from the global transportation network.

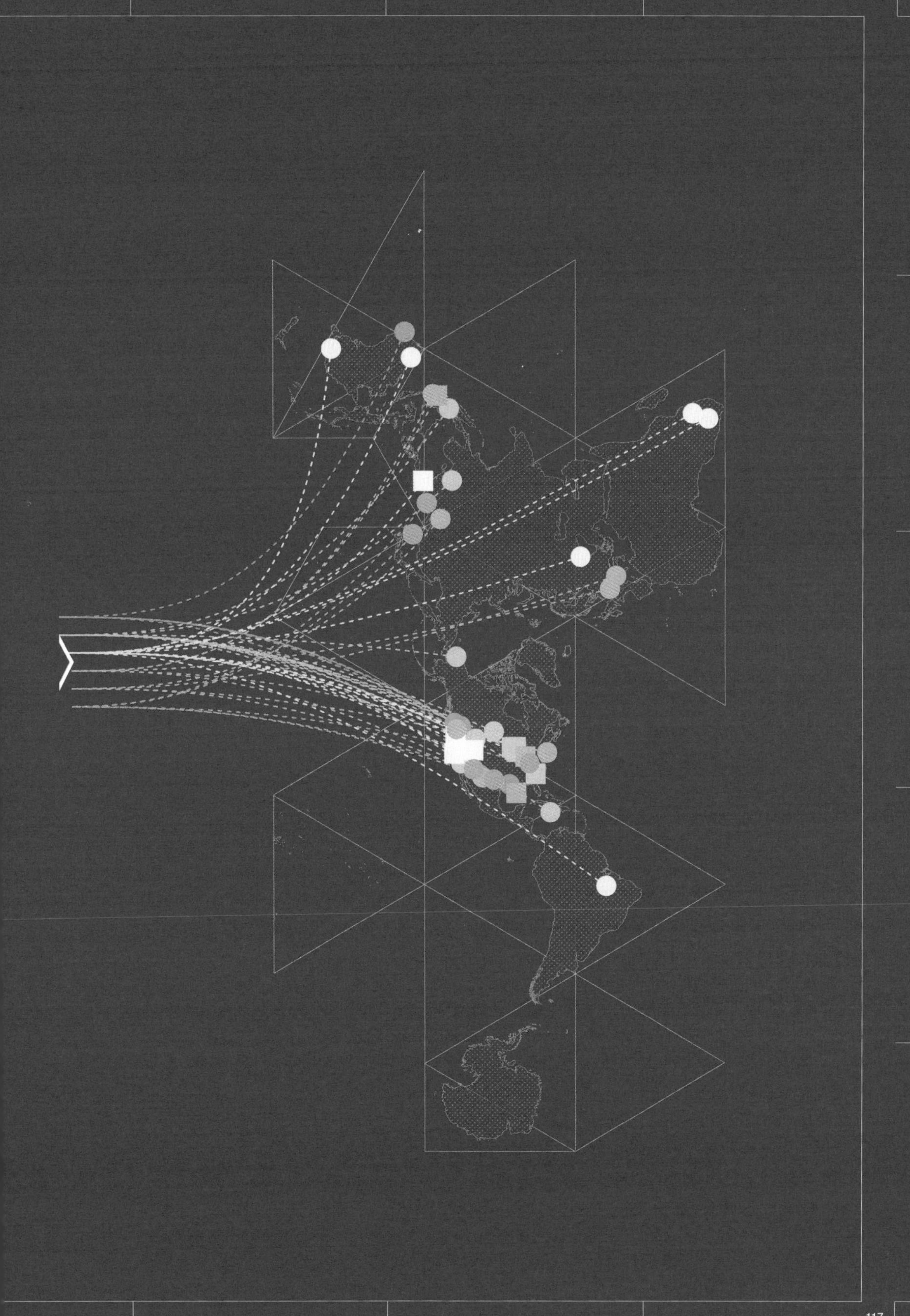

David Trigger works on the different meanings attributed to land and nature across diverse sectors of society and in different countries. He is an emeritus professor in the School of Social Science at the University of Queensland.

"Ethnography is no longer 'built upon the idea of little worlds in and of themselves', as if they were discrete loci of social activity.... the trend toward such work has been prompted by the notion of 'repatriating' anthropological endeavour, through the key strategy of 'defamiliarization', whereby insights gained on 'the periphery of the Euro-centric world' are brought 'back to the center'."

The decisiveness of the final building, its gravitational hold on the earth, belies the tangled web of realities that made it happen. For that reason, we need to always remind ourselves of the strange inversion that is in play here. While the possibility of intelligibility is presented throughout the profession and discipline (promised in the very idea of 'research' even if it is the pre-condition of intelligibility), the house seeks to preserve the secret that is at its core—at the core of its very sense of modernity—the mythic violence/productivity that makes it possible.

There is no Archimedean point by which one can understand the modernity of this house. Not in the history of its aesthetics, materials, labor, or even in its self-professed critiques. And yet the building as it stands in the landscape is not a contradiction. On the contrary, it speaks unambiguously. But about what? The more one studies it, or—better stated—fights against its foreclosures, the more one realizes it has an almost magical place in contemporary culture. But if in one breath it is magical, in the next it is scandalous.

Concrete

The concrete mix used for the house was manufactured by Salmon Bay Sand & Gravel Company, located in Seattle. The cumulative distance from each of the locations from which raw materials were sourced and processed (such as the Cascade Quarry, Lafarge Quarry, and Coalmont Mine), to Salmon Bay's Seattle branch, is 3,269 miles. Given the highly varied distribution of mineral deposits across the United States and North America, and the fact that most material processing happens in close proximity to extraction sites, such vast transportation networks are ubiquitous within the concrete industry.

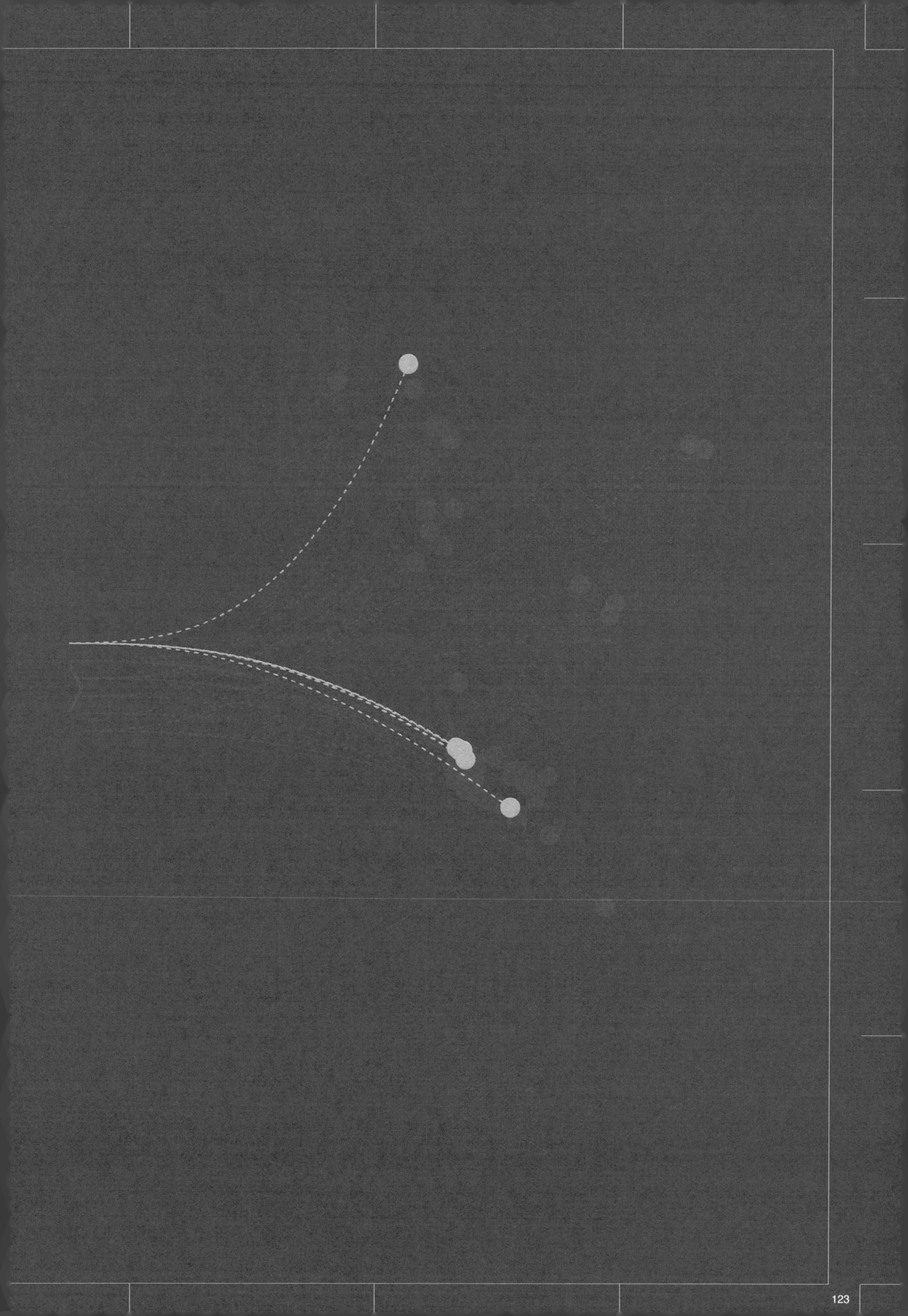

Limestone I Lafarge Quarry

The Lafarge Quarry in Texada, British Columbia, Canada, from which the limestone was sourced, is the oldest active mine in the province. It produces an average of four million tons of limestone per year. The limestone is barged to Lafarge's Seattle facility for processing into a general-use Portland cement, and subsequently shipped to retailers around the globe. According to the United States Geological Survey (USGS), the majority of limestone's cost to the customer is determined by the distance and means of transportation, given that it is considered a low-value, high-volume commodity. Shipping by barge is the most cost-effective, and therefore the most prevalent, means of transporting limestone in the world, with transportation via truck being the least favorable option.

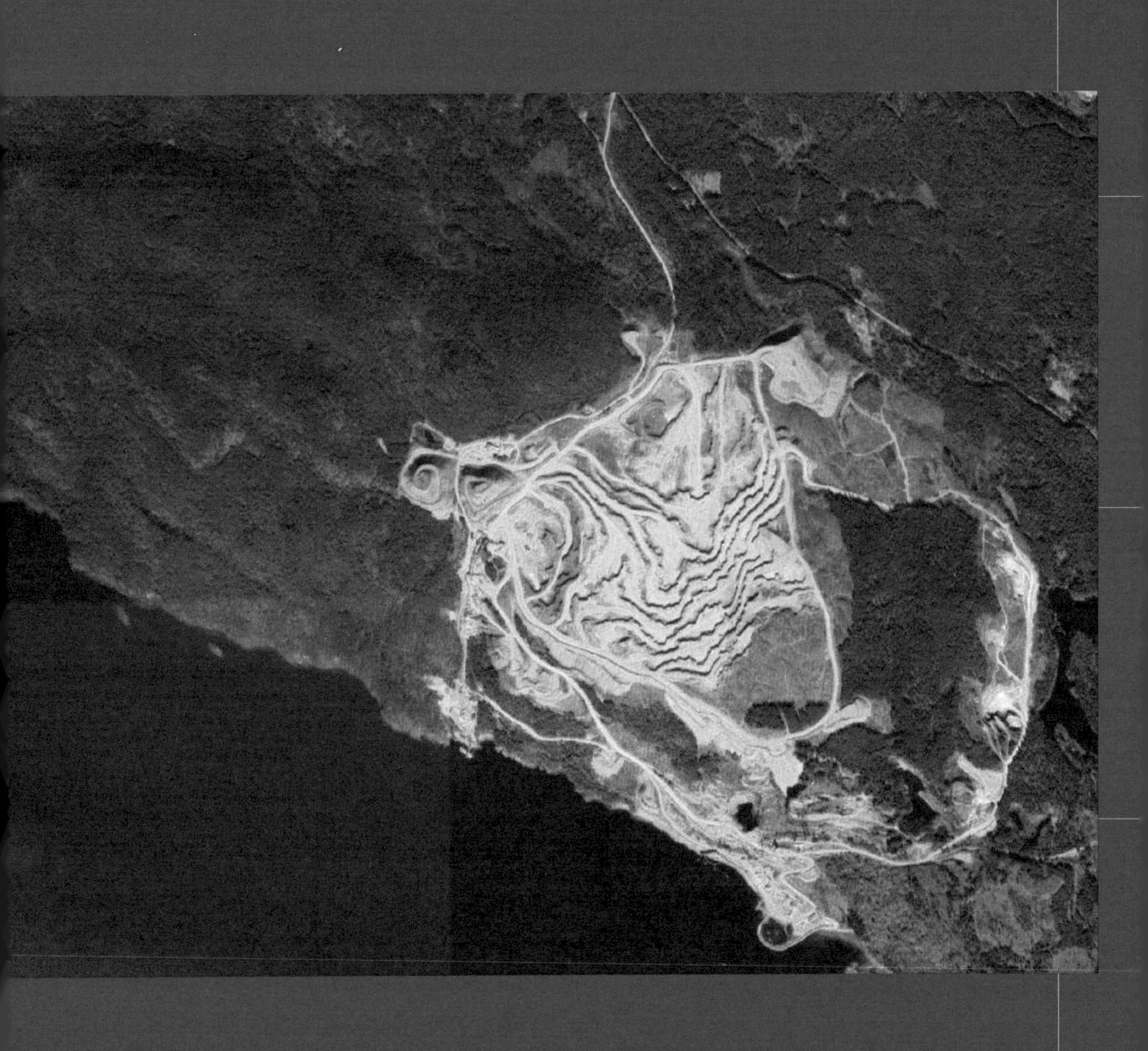

+ *The Lafarge Quarry, on Texada Island in British Columbia, Canada, with imagery ©2022 CNES / Airbus, IMTCAN, Landsat / Copernicus, Maxar Technologies. Map data ©2022.*

Aggregate | Cascade Quarry

The aggregate used in the Seattle house—a mixture of sand and gravel—was originally sourced from the Cascade Quarry, located just outside the city as part of CalPortland's facility in the town of Gold Bar, WA. It can be speculated that, due to large-sized gravel particles, increasing the quantity of water required to maintain the workability of wet concrete, and given that a water-reducing admixture was incorporated into the mix used in the house, relatively small-sized gravel particles were used as the coarse aggregate. In compliance with Washington State Department of Transportation (WSDOT) transport specifications, the gravel used was likely classified as 5/8" Minus Quarry Rock (i.e., gravel with a diameter of 5/8" or less).

The US aggregate industry comprises approximately 3870 mining companies for sand and gravel across all fifty states. The top ten producing states by tonnage, of which Washington ranks sixth, accounted for 55% of all national aggregate production in 2019.

The Cascade Quarry, in Gold Bar, WA, with imagery ©2022 Maxar Technologies, U.S. Geological Survey, USDA/FPAC/GEO. Map data ©2022.

Fly Ash | Basin Coal Mine

While the use of fly ash as a partial replacement for cement in concrete does reduce some of the CO_2 emissions associated with processing raw materials into cement, the compound presents a host of environmental problems, mainly due to disposal methods. The fly ash added to the cement mixture used in the house was sourced from Coalmont Energy Corp.'s Basin Coal Mine, located in British Columbia. In 2013, 1060 cubic feet of sludge from Coalmont's tailings pond entered the Tulameen River, sparking outrage from the residents of Coalmont.

Fly ash represents a tangible, material link between the fossil fuel industry and the construction industry—its use reinforces a paradigm of coal-based energy.

The Basin Coal Mine, in Tulameen, British Columbia, Canada, with imagery ©2022 CNES / Airbus, Maxar Technologies, Province of British Columbia. Map data ©2022.

Admixtures | BASF

The admixtures were supplied by the Texas branch of BASF, one of the largest producers of chemicals and related products in North America.

The use of admixtures can be traced back to some of the first uses of concrete itself—the Roman Empire has been found to have used milk, blood, and lard to alter the physical and chemical properties of its concrete. The admixtures that are more familiar to us today (accelerators, air-entrainers, etc.) were first used in North America in the 1930s, and were gradually popularized over the next two decades.

\+ *BASF facilities in Freeport, TX, with imagery ©2022 Houston-Galveston Area Council, Maxar Technologies, Texas General Land Office, U.S. Geological Survey, USDA/FPAC/GEO. Map data ©2022.*

Glass

The new glass installed in the house was manufactured by Wisconsin-based Cardinal Glass, with window assemblies by Kolbe Windows and Velux Skylights. The existing windows are by Anderson Eagle, with glass that comes from three possible sources, one of which is Cardinal Glass. Given that the primary materials of glass have an incredibly low cost-to-weight ratio and are uneconomical to transport over long distances, glass is typically made as close as possible to the manufacturer's chosen supply of sand.

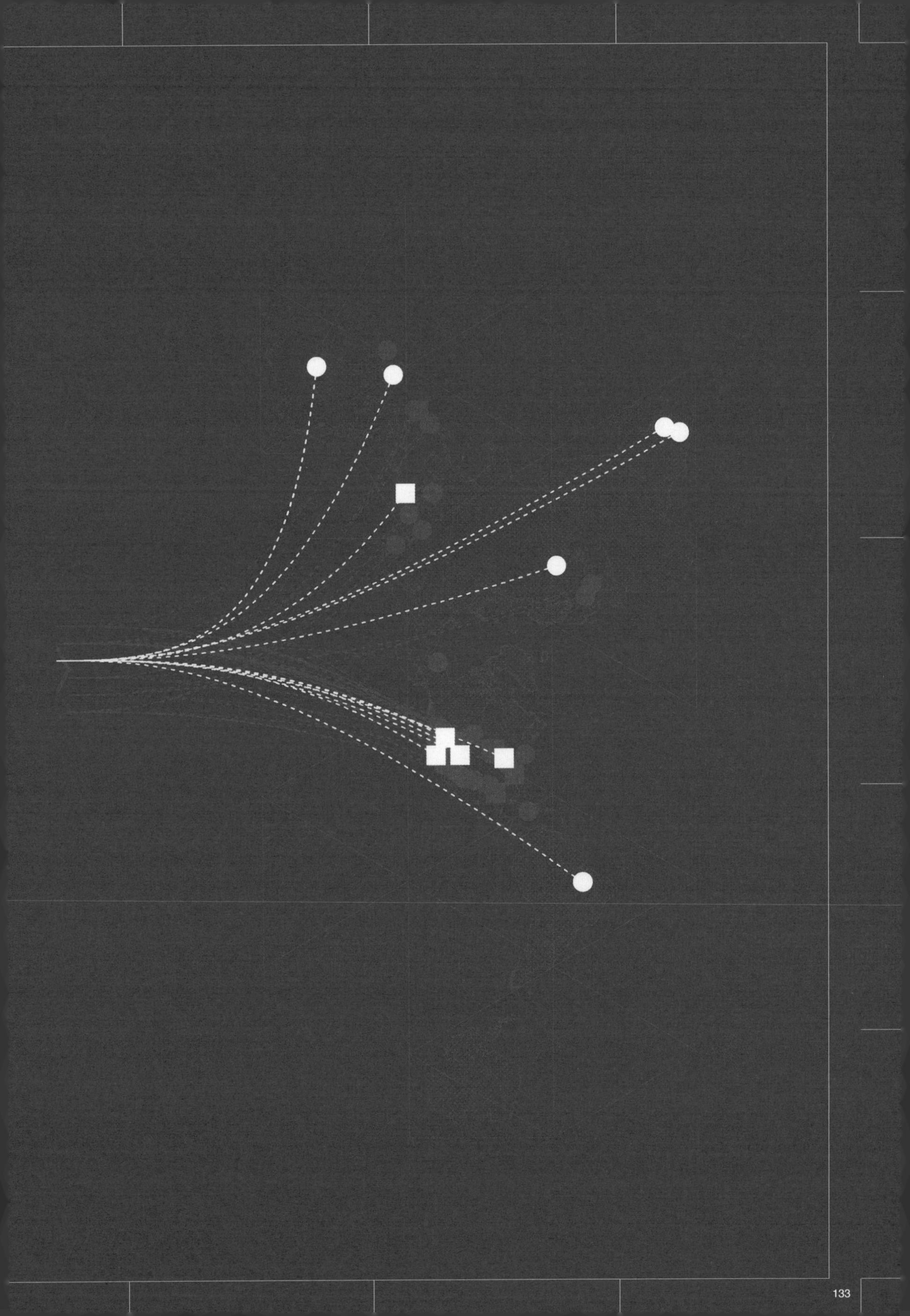

Tin Oxide | Bangka Belitung Islands

Although tin is not an ingredient in the manufacturing of glass, it is a vital material when the material's production methods are considered. A fundamental process in the production of glass, described in a subsequent section, involves floating molten glass over a bed of molten tin. It is this process that allows us to create the now ubiquitous flat panes of glass. As tin is one of the only known, economically viable materials that is denser than glass when both are in their liquid form, there is currently no viable substitute for it.

In the United States, where Cardinal Glass is based, there is roughly a 75–78% net import reliance for tin, as no tin has been mined or smelted within the country since 1993 and 1989, respectively. Recycled tin from scrap and reclaimed metals account for the remaining supply. Of these sources—domestic and imported—however, the primary source is imports from Indonesia, where stunningly, all recorded sources of tin by the USGS are in the Bangka Islands and the surrounding region.

The islands' inland tin mines have closed over time, so mining has moved to the coastline and the seabed off the Bangka Belitung Islands.

Due to the more inland position of the Wisconsin glass factories, it is likely that recycled, refined tin is used in the production of the glass in the house. That said, if current patterns of consumption and import hold true, it is likely that the original tin came from Indonesia, followed by Malaysia, or Peru. China is actually the world's top producer of tin, but just barely, exceeding Indonesia's output by about 1%.

+ *The Sungai Liat Coast of Indonesia's Bangka Belitung Islands, by Fabio Achilli (Flickr)*

Lead Oxide | Fletcher Mine

Lead oxide is another compound commonly added to glass, although in carefully controlled amounts. The compound can increase the chemical resistance of glass, but too much lead lowers the melting temperature and decreases its hardness. Historically, lead has seen more significant use in glass for decorative purposes, and in tableware.

A majority of the lead used in the United States comes from domestic sources, more specifically, from six mines in Missouri and five in the states of Alaska, Idaho, and Washington. While the Red Dog Mine in Alaska is the largest producer of lead in the form of zinc-lead ore, lead for glass manufacturing in Wisconsin would more probably have been from the runner-up, the Fletcher Mine in Reynolds, MO. Owned and operated by the Doe Run Resources Corporation of St Louis—the nation's largest lead producer—lead ore would be mined and subsequently processed at a smelter within the state.

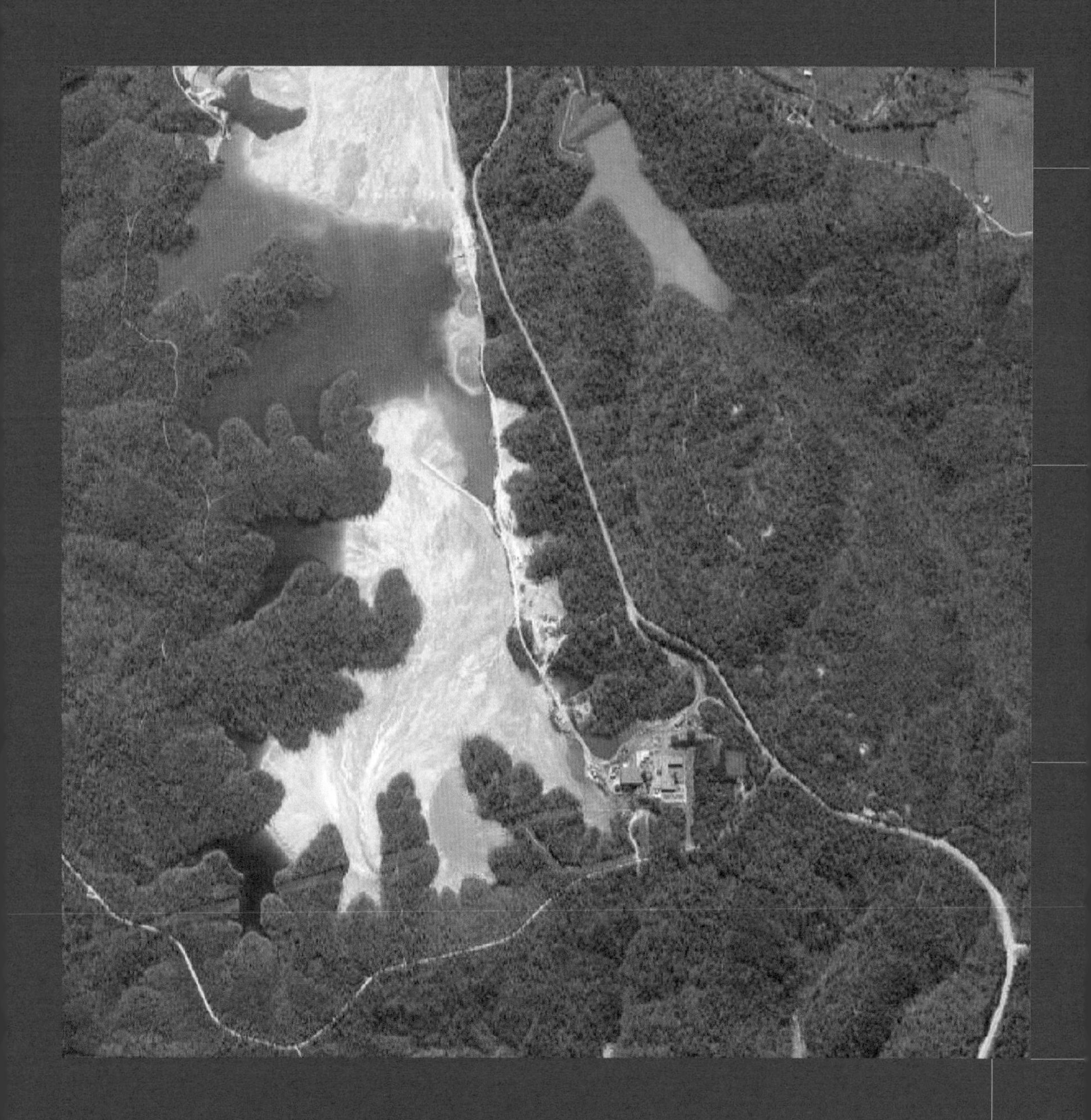

\+ *Fletcher Mine, in Reynolds, MO, with imagery ©2022 Maxar Technologies, USDA/FPAC/GEO. Map data ©2022.*

Glass Windows I Cardinal Glass

Started in 1962 by M.L. Gordon in Minneapolis, Minnesota, Cardinal Glass today is a $2.1 bilion industry that manufacgures in more than 22 plants across the US, with about 7,000 employees. It is a privately held company with Roger O'Shaughnessy the majority owner with 60%, with the rest held by about 50 employees.Cardinal pioneered lightweight, energy-efficient windows in the late 1970s and early 1980s. They have a reputation for producing glass products with some of the best thermal performance and lowest failure rates in the industry.

+ *Cardinal Glass Factory, Menomonie, WI, with imagery ©2022 Maxar Technologies, USDA/FPAC/GEO. Map data ©2022.*

Boron Oxide | Searles Lake, Mojave Desert

Although primarily used in the production of optical glass, boron oxide is another stabilizer that is often added to the basic glass batch. As the number of borate producers in the United States is limited, most of the trade data related to borates is withheld to prevent loss of proprietary data. We do know, however, that most of the borate products in the United States are manufactured locally, and the two largest producers are located in Southern California.

Searles Lake sits in the Mojave Desert, in northwestern San Bernadino County in California. The mining facilities built around the dry lake process its brine by evaporating its waters, yielding borate minerals along with sodium and potassium minerals. Both the major companies that process boron in the United States also own rail systems to transport their products to intermediaries and manufacturing facilities.

The mineral wealth of this area is so vast that the California Office of Historic Preservation estimates that the formation contains at least "half the natural elements known to man."

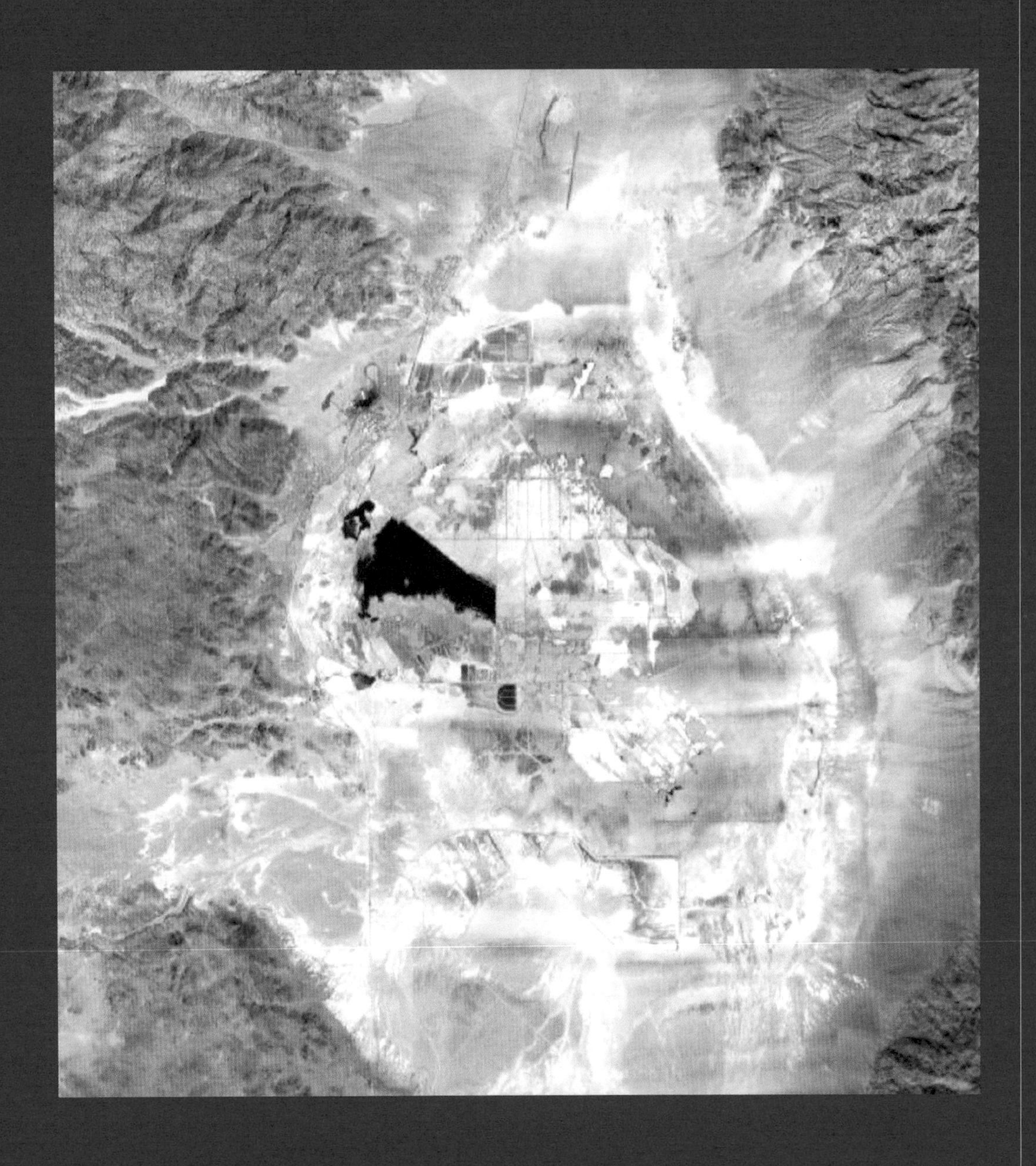

+ *Searles Lake in California's Mojave Desert, with imagery ©2022 TerraMetrics. Map data ©2022.*

Sand | Covia Mine

The highly specific requirements for industrial sand mean that the viability of high quality glass manufacturing is mostly dictated by access to the required geological formations with that sand. The cost inefficiencies of transporting the sand usually also mean that in areas that would incur high transport and labor cost, glass is usually just imported. In the United States, for example, glass from Europe is a viable option for the East Coast, and glass from China and Japan is similarly so for locations along the West Coast.

Cardinal Glass, however, bucks the trend with a production network based primarily in the United States. With relatively easy access to the Wisconsin sandstones, the company has invested in multiple facilities in the Badger State, from sand mines and processing, to float glass plants and coating plants. The particular mine that the sand is sourced from is most likely the Covia (and formerly Fairmount) mine in Menomonie, WI, from which it travels a short distance by truck to the Cardinal Float Glass facility in the same town. Most of the primary materials, such as lime and soda, would also be transported to the same locations, but via rail from Wyoming and Montana.

+ *Covia Mine, in Menomonie, WI, with imagery ©2022 CNES / Airbus, Maxar Technologies, USDA/FPAC/GEO. Map data ©2022.*

Sand I Taylor Frac Mine

The sand mining in Wisconsin is not done exclusively for industrial sand for glass, but rather, the sand is available for glass as a co-product with the search for another specific type of sand—frac sand. In what has been called Wisconsin's "Sand Rush," the state has become the epicenter of coordinated efforts to explore, drill into, and fracture land to access its sandstone formations. It is this demand for frac sand that has made the sourcing of sand for glass economically viable in Wisconsin. The United States is estimated by NASA to be the largest global consumer of industrial sand (a category that includes the sand used for fracking and glass-making), with roughly 63% of it used for fracking, and with glass production creating the next largest demand for it.

To extract this sand, companies must first remove the "overburden"—the topsoil over the sand deposit—before proceeding with a combination of machinery and blasting. The sand then needs to be washed, dried, and sorted, before it is stockpiled in large heaps to await transport. The pace of this extraction has largely been in pace with the demand for oil and increased hydraulic fracture mining, often bringing into conflict the companies that are on the search for new lands to mine and the existing farming communities that rely upon the land.

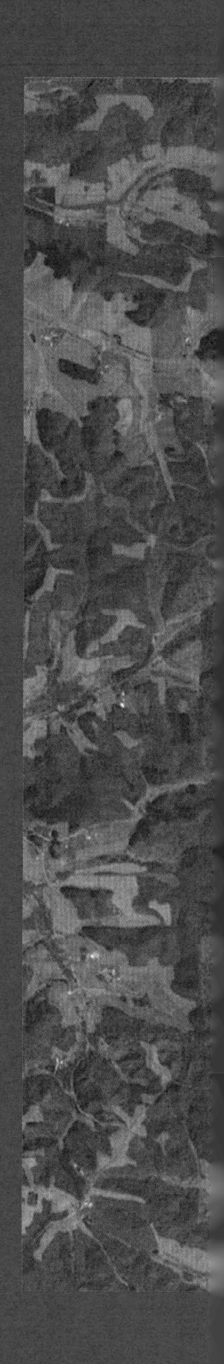

+ *Taylor Frac Mine in Wisconsin, with imagery ©2022 Landsat / Copernicus, Maxar Technologies, USDA/FPAC/GEO. Map data ©2022.*

Trona I Green River Formation

The second major component by mass in glass is soda, or sodium oxide, derived from sodium carbonate. Sodium carbonate is primarily produced through the Solvay process, in an intricate reaction of limestone, ammonia and concentrated brine. (The process is identical to that which would be used for making baking soda.) However, an accidental discovery in 1938, by the Mountain Fuel Supply Company, has actually resulted in a naturally occurring alternative for the United States, in the form of trona. In their search for oil, the company actually chanced upon a sample of the Green River Formation in Wyoming, the largest known formation of trona in the world. This formation is so extensive, that it is now responsible for 90% of the United States' production of the mineral, and at current rates of consumption, is expected to last for over 2000 years. With an estimated 127 billion tons of the sodium carbonate mineral within relatively easy access, this has allowed for an abundant, economical supply of soda for both glass manufacturing and baking soda in the United States. A portion of this trona would have been processed and transported by rail from Wyoming to Wisconsin for the glass used in the Seattle house.

Following the extinction of the dinosaurs 65 million years ago, this area of Wyoming was host to a crocodile infested lake, rich in marine life and surrounded by forests and active volcanoes. Volcanic ash buried dead trees in anaerobic conditions which eventually, with shifting continental plates, resulted in the green trona that is mined today to make calcium carbonate.

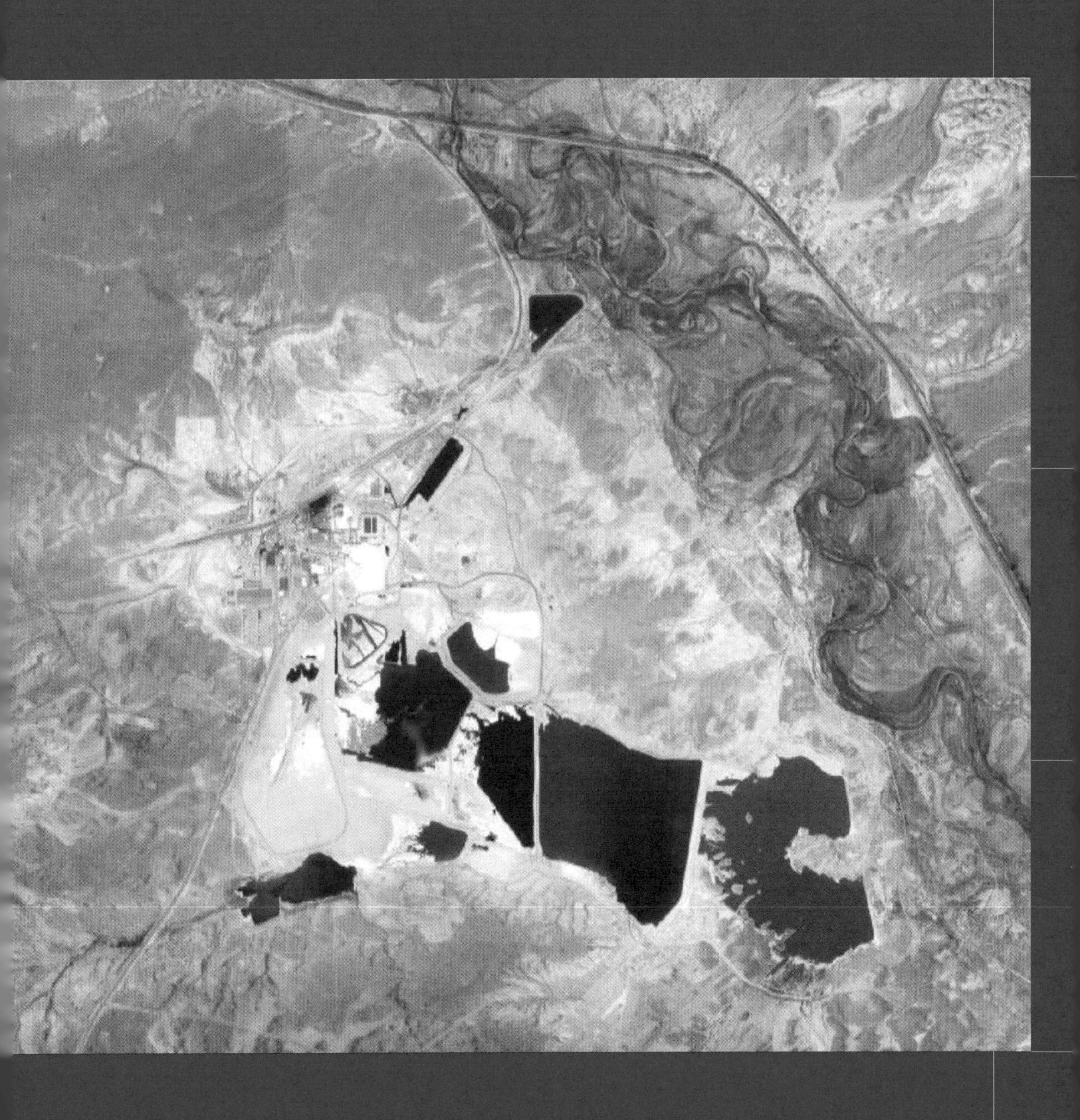

+ *Alchem Trona Mine, Green River Formation, in Wyoming, with imagery ©2022 Landsat / Copernicus, Maxar Technologies, USDA/FPAC/GEO. Map data ©2022.*

Dolomite | Regal Mine

The dolomite in the sourcing of lime is also used in glass production to introduce magnesium oxide into the glass batch. It is available globally in similar quantities to limestone, and would most likely be simultaneously sourced from the Madison Group in Montana.

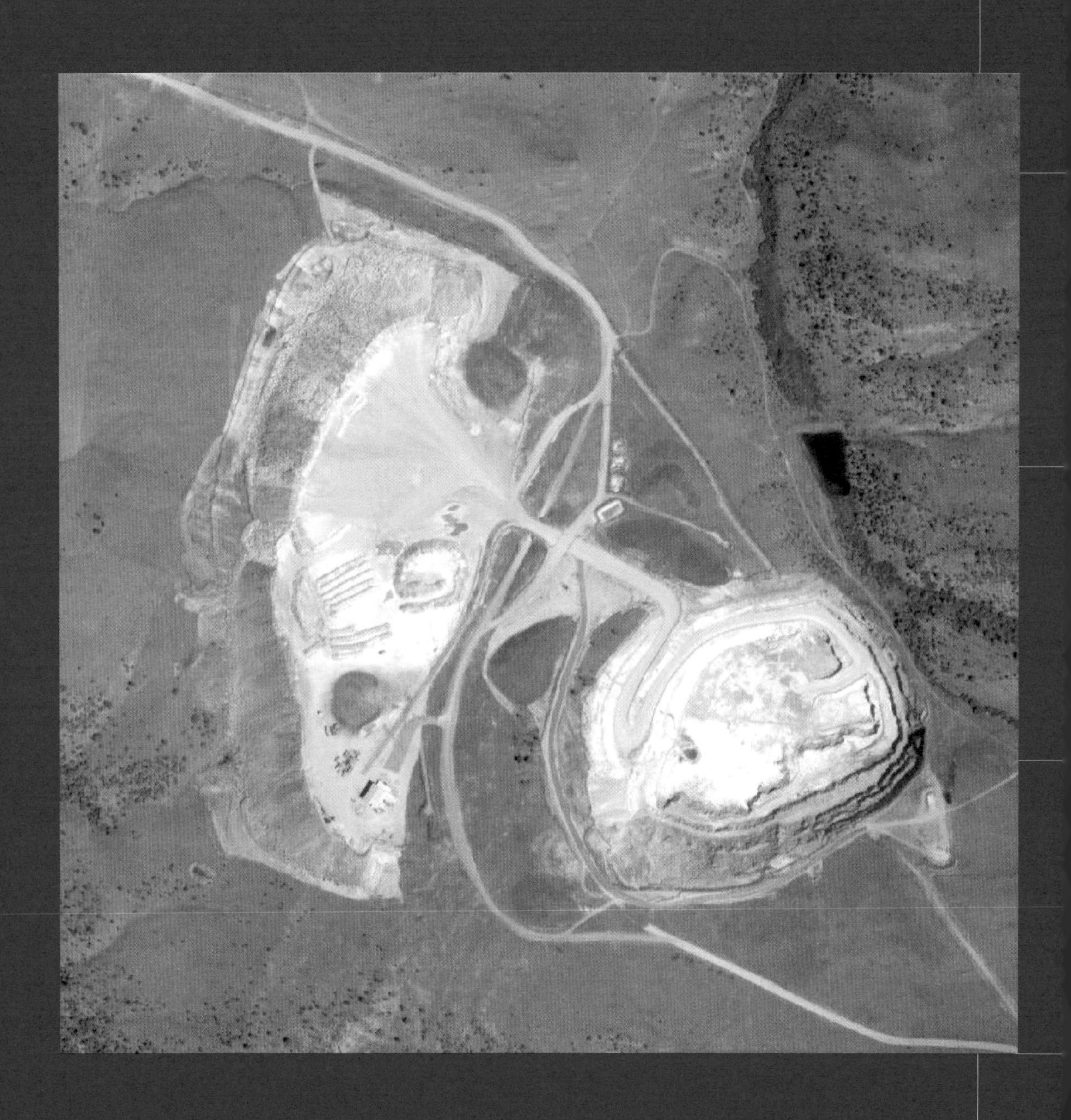

+ *Regal Mine in Montana, with imagery ©2022 Maxar Technologies, USDA/FPAC/GEO. Map data ©2022.*

Bauxite | Nain Mine

Aluminum oxide is the most common stabilizer added to glass, in addition to the basic ingredient of lime. While aluminum for most manufacturing might benefit from recycled sources of the metal, the metallurgical-grade alumina required for glass production is almost entirely imported into the United States, and brought into the country as refined alumina, or processed from mineral bauxite. Much of the aluminum production within the United States is focused on non-metallurgical purposes, such as in the manufacturing of abrasives, cement, and chemicals.

Of the bauxite imported into the United States, just over 50% of it originates from mines in Jamaica. The largest of these mines is in St. Elizabeth, Nain, and is owned by JISCO, a Chinese state-owned mining giant that recently acquired it from the Russian aluminum company RUSAL.

Aluminum is the most abundant metal in the earth's crust, mostly because it is lighter and floats up (unlike nickel and iron which, being heavier, sink down towards the core of the earth). It occurs as bauxite and cryolite. Bauxite is ground and mixed with lime and sodium hydroxide and heated to produce aluminum oxide.

Jamaica's Nain Mine is seeking to expand its mining base.

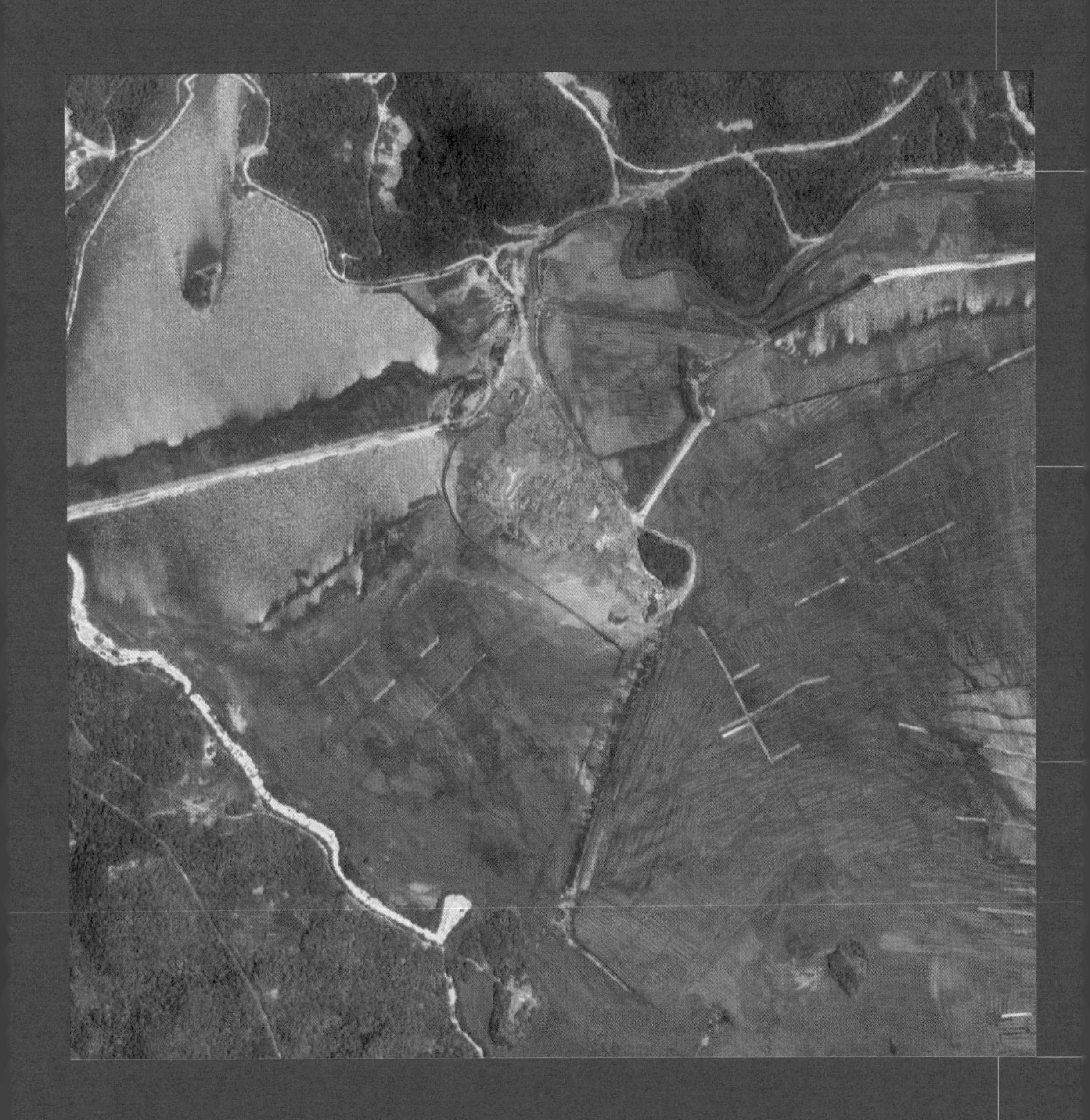

\+ Nain Mine in Nain, Jamaica, with imagery ©2022 CNES / Airbus, Maxar Technologies. Map data ©2022.

Lime | Graymont Limestone Quarry

The lime used in the production of Cardinal Glass for the Seattle house has a much less specific story than the soda and industrial sand. Lime is primarily mined from limestone and dolomite, where it exists as calcium carbonate and calcium magnesium carbonate. These stones are found in relatively common formations of sedimentary rock and are also mined to produce other construction materials, such as cladding stone, concrete, and paint.

While China is the largest global producer of lime by more than a factor of 10, there are over 1400 companies and 3600 limestone mines across the United States, and untapped limestone resources are so abundant that the United States is completely self reliant for it by all estimates of current and projected use. The most likely source of the limestone used in the glass at the Seattle house, as mentioned in interviews and company profiles, is the Madison Limestone Formation, or Madison Group, made accessible via railroads from Montana to Wisconsin.

+ *Graymont Quarry in Montana, with imagery ©2022 CNES / Airbus, Maxar Technologies. Map data ©2022.*

Potash | Mosaic Potash Mine

Of the all basic ingredients for glass, potash is the one material that is most likely to be imported to the United States. With a 88–91% net import reliance over the last five years, most of the potash needed in the United States for not only glass production, but other products such as fertilizers and manufactured salts, comes from international sources. Fortunately for Cardinal Glass production in Wisconsin, one need not go too far for the largest potash mining industry in the world.

The Canadian province of Saskatchewan is home to about a dozen potash mines and an estimated 45% of the world's reserve of the mineral. The Prairie Evaporite Formation that contains all this potash stretches right across Saskatchewan, and into the US states of Montana and North Dakota. This geological formation is the result of the evaporation of an inland sea around 328 million years ago during the Middle Devonian Period, and can be found at depths of up to 950 meters below the ground. As most of the minerals in the formation are water-soluble, nearly none of the formation can be seen in outcrops.

This need to mine for potash at depth produces a very distinct type of mine in the landscape. Conventional mining involves excavation to a few hundred meters below ground, where a labyrinth of tunnels and rooms allow for the extraction of the sylvinite ore that contains potash. More recently, however, solution mining has provided a useful alternative to access deeper deposits of potash. In this process, wells are dug deep into the ground and into the potash deposits. Hot brine is then pumped into these wells to dissolve the potash and bring it up to the surface. The brine is then evaporated to extract the potash. As a result of this, solution mines are usually also accompanied by large, brightly colored pools, where the potash solution is dyed using bright colors to increase its evaporation rate.

"Potash" as a term derives from "pot-ash" a preindustrial process that was used to make it from plant ash that was processed in pots.

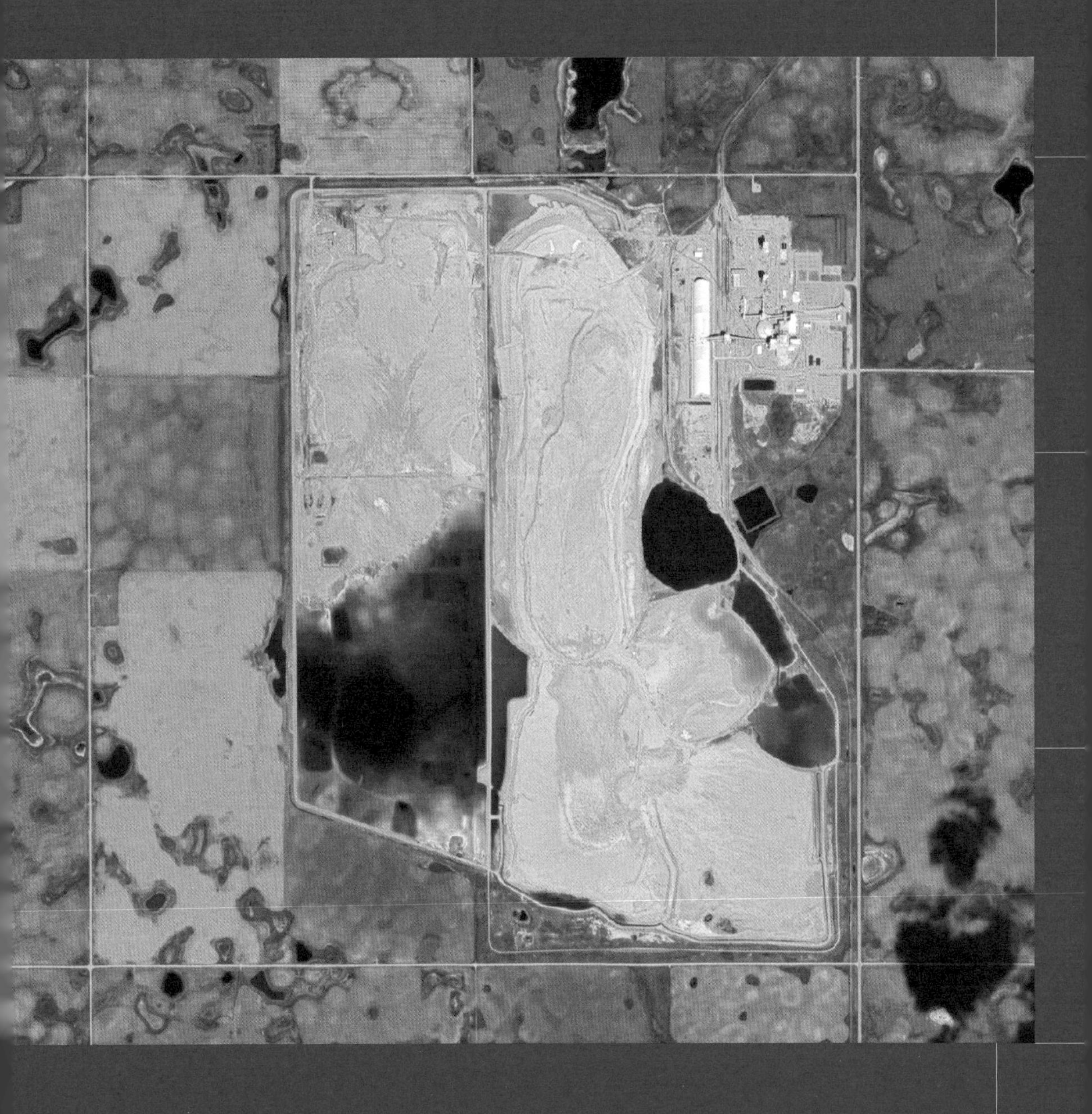

+ *Mosaic Potash Mine in Saskatchewan, Canada, with imagery ©2022 CNES / Airbus, Maxar Technologies. Map data ©2022.*

Steel

The main elements of steel are iron, carbon, manganese, chromium, phosphorous, sulfur, nickel, molybdenum, titanium, copper, and boron.

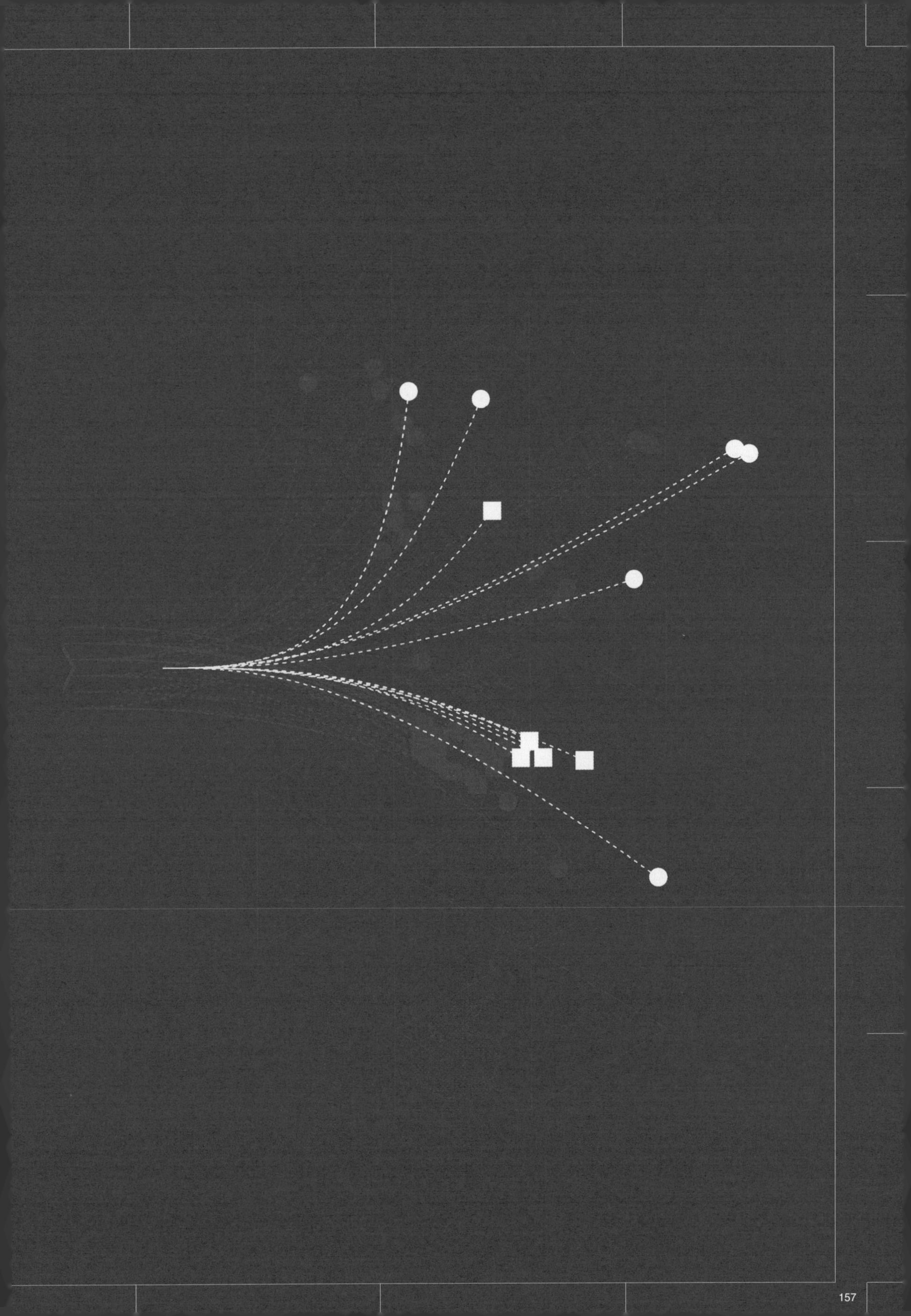

Iron Ore | Black Iron Mine

Iron is the main ingredient in steel, and is smelted from iron ore. Iron mining produced 48 million metric tons of iron ore in 2019, and is the third highest metal mined in the United States. It is mined in Michigan, Minnesota, and Utah.

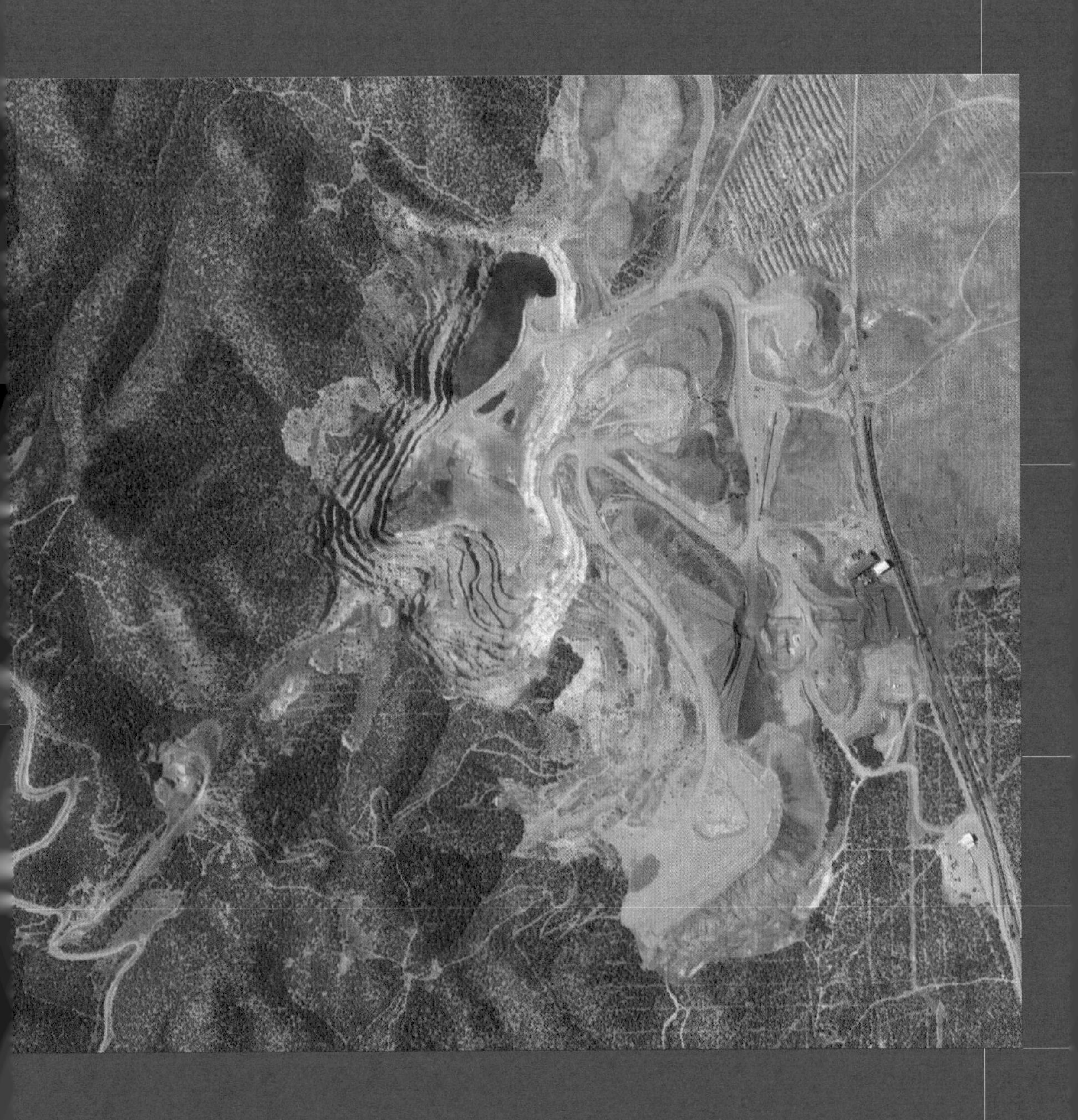

+ *Black Iron Mine in Utah, with imagery ©2022 Maxar Technologies, State of Utah, USDA/FPAC/GEO. Map data ©2022.*

Coking Coal | Warrior Met Coal Mine

Carbon is added to iron in order to increase the steel's strength. Coking coal produces coke, the form of carbon needed for this process. Coking coal is different than thermal coal in that it typically has higher energy content and lower moisture levels, and is from hard coal not low rank coal. In the United States, Alabama, Arkansas, Virginia, and West Virginia produce coking coal from their mines.

+ *Warrior Met Coal Mine in Alabama, with imagery ©2022 Maxar Technologies, USDA/FPAC/GEO. Map data ©2022.*

Steel I Northwest Steel and Pipe

Steel was sourced from Northwest Steel and Pipe in Tacoma, WA (just south of Seattle) and fabricated into the staircase at Bear Creek Metal in Bothell (just north of Seattle).

Northwest Steel and Pipe, Inc. is a small local family owned and operated business, now in its third generation of ownership. It started in 1950 as scrap metal and salvage yard, and transformed into a steel business in the 1970s. They operate out of a 160,000 sq. ft. facility in South Tacoma, Washington.

Northwest Steel and Pipe in Washington, with imagery ©2022 CNES / Airbus, Maxar Technologies, U.S. Geological Survey. Map data ©2022.

Wood

Wood is a primary ingredient of the Seattle house. As previously discussed, it made its way to the building in three forms: lumber in the house structure, plywood in its partitions, and aggregated in its parquet flooring. The lumber and plywood are mainly made of Douglas fir coming from the United States, the parquet's white oak is sourced in Germany and its softwood filling is grown in Indonesia.

Timber exploitation has far from an equitable past. This largely comes from different ethnic groups having varying relationships to land property and forest sustainability. At the center of this cultural divide is the question of whether trees are valuable as an extracted resource (to produce lumber upon which industrialized economies rely) or as an ecological resource (supporting thriving fauna and flora ecosystems upon which locals often rely).

The Worldwide Fund for Nature says the earth is losing its forest cover at the rate of a football field every two seconds. An estimated 10% of all man-made greenhouse gas emissions are caused by deforestation, much of which is due to illegal logging.

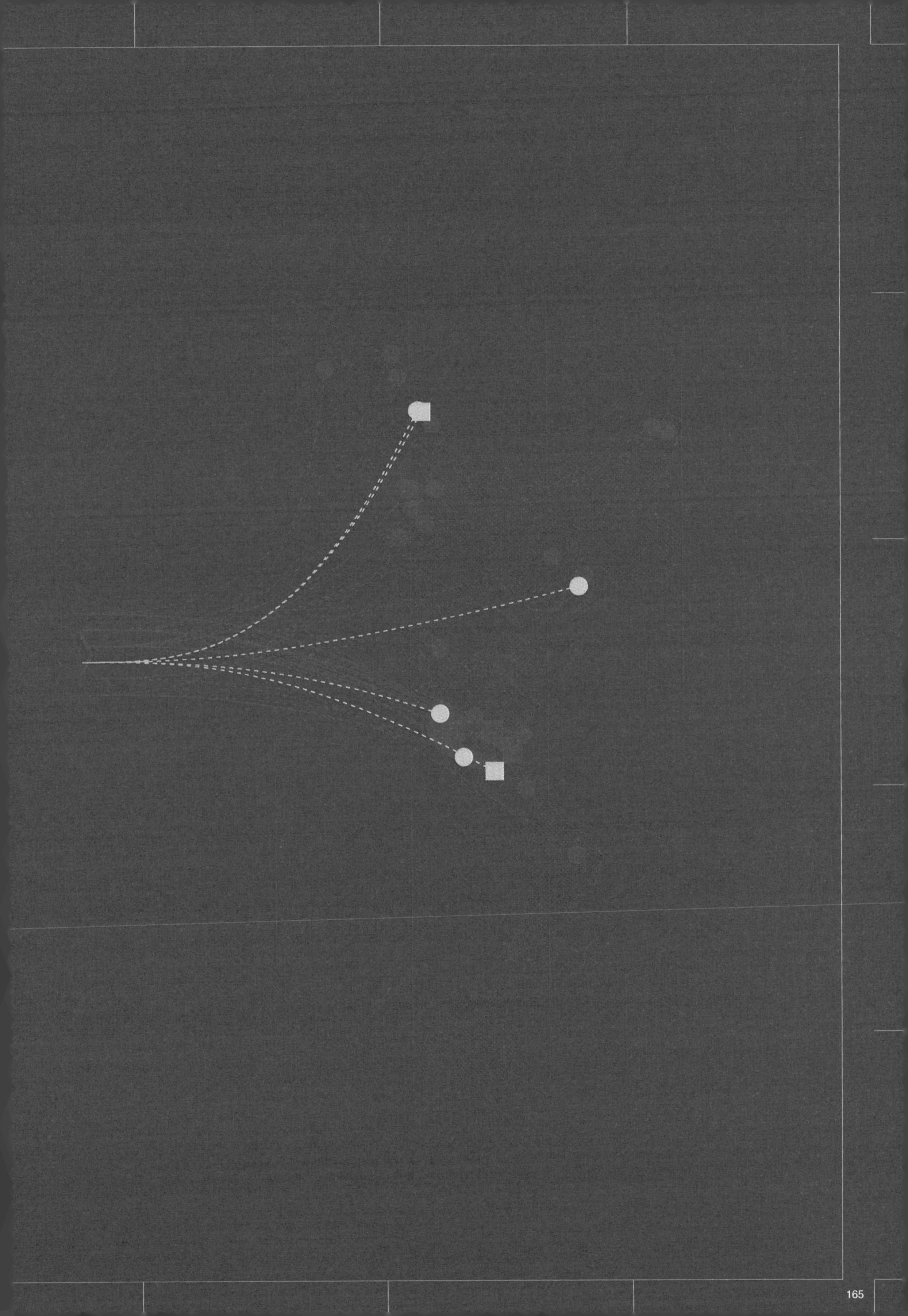

Douglas Fir Lumber I Washington

Wood is a primary ingredient of the Seattle house. It made its way to the house in three forms, lumber in the house structure, plywood in its partitions, and aggregated in its parquet flooring. Lumber was sourced from the Oregon Lumber Company. The lumber and plywood are mainly made of Douglas fir coming from the United States, while the parquet's white oak is sourced in Germany and its softwood filling is grown in Indonesia.

Oregon Lumber Company is a local family-owned operation in service since 1962. In 2019 the Oregon lumber companies reached an agreement with local environmental organizations to develop a statewide conservation plan for endangered species, on pesticide notifications and buffers for streams.

FSC PEFC

There are several certification labels available in Germany. The Bonn-based (Germany) juggernaut Forest Stewardship Council (FSC), created in 1993, is one of them. FSC is an international non-profit and multi-stakeholder organization trying to promote responsible management of the world's forests. After years of acclamation, former founder, Simon Counsell, left the organization, claiming that FSC has severe problems of traceability, affordability, and equity. Counsell pointed, for example, at the cumbersome and expensive certification process that tends to favor significantly larger corporations leaving no options to small owners.

FSC's certification of products from 'mixed sources,' which "allows up to 90% of the wood fiber in some FSC-labeled products to come from forests or plantations that are not FSC-certified, is also a concerning issue. According to Counsell, "the Mixed Sources policy is allowing the laundering of unacceptable wood into the FSC system."

As the trust in FSC started to deplete, the Program for the Endorsement of Forest Certification (PEFC) was created in 1999 and became the norm in the country. Today, it is estimated that 7% of German forests are certified according to FSC standards and 65% according to PEFC..

+ *Forests just outside Oso, WA, with imagery ©2022 Maxar Technologies, U.S. Geological Survey, USDA/FPAC/GEO. Map data ©2022.*

White Oak Flooring | Spessart Forest

Spessart Oak quarter cut wood veneer grows exclusively in the carefully maintained forests of Bavaria, Germany. It is usually referred to as "gold standard" amongst the oaks. Maintaining this "gold standard" requires extensive soil managment, including carefully orchestrated drainage.

German forestry dates to the early 1800s. Since white oak seedlings need a lot of light to grow, foresters thinned them until only the best were left. Under them they then planted beech trees which grow well in the shade of the oak. Three generations of beech trees are harvested before the oak matures. It takes a Spessart oak three hundred to four hundred years or more to mature.

\+ *The Spessart Forest in Bavaria, Germany, with imagery ©2022 GeoBasis-DE/BKG, GeoContent, Maxar Technologies. Map data ©2022.*

Lumber | Oregon Industrial Lumber Products

Wood is a primary ingredient of the Deconstructed House. It made its way to the house in three forms, lumber in the house structure, plywood in its partitions, and aggregated in its parquet flooring. Lumber was sourced from the Oregon Lumber Company. The lumber and plywood are mainly made of Douglas fir coming from the United States of America, the parquet's white oak is sourced in Germany and its softwood filling is grown in Indonesia.

Oregon Industrial Lumber Products is family owned, and about 60 years old.

+ *Oregon Industrial Lumber Products in Oregon, with imagery ©2022 CNES / Airbus, Maxar Technologies, State of Oregon. Map data ©2022.*

Ceramics

The 2.55 tons of tile in the house were purchased from Contract Furnishings Mart, located in Seattle. Contract Furnishings, however, sourced the tiles from Caesar Ceramiche, a company located in Florence, whose design, research, and production work (including milling, spray drying, pressing, decoration, and firing) all occurs within Italy. Thus, while both the site of production and that of commerce/retail have a strong sense of locality, the fact that they exist within a global network means that the cumulative travel distance of the Seattle house's tiles was 8800 km.

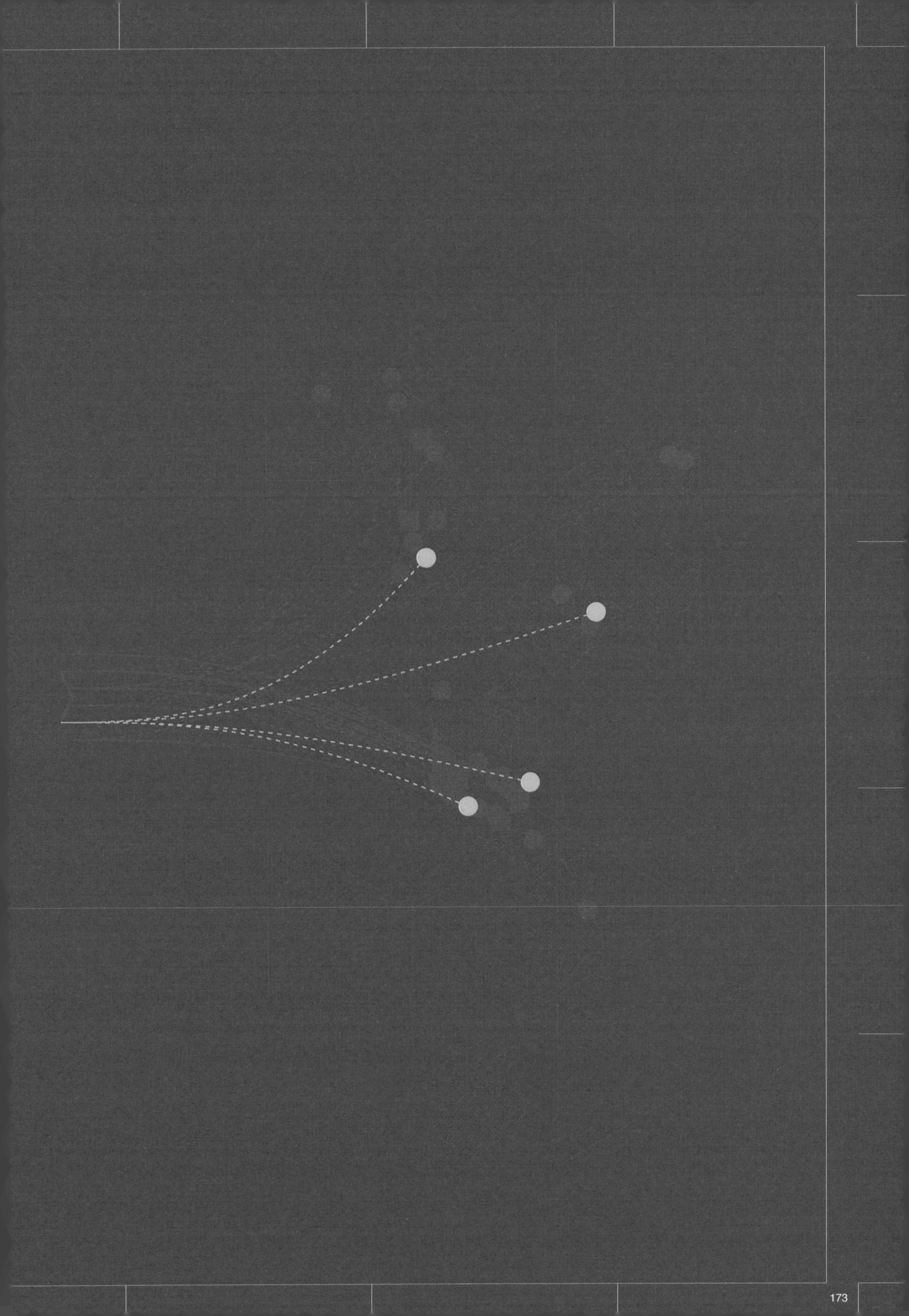

Tiles | Caesar Ceramiche

75% of Caesar Ceramiche's locally produced tile is exported to over 200 countries, which suggests that transportation costs on the consumer end constitute a significant portion of the product's cost.

Caesar Ceramics designs its products in Italy intended significantly for the United States market. Manufacturing is done in the United States.

+ *Caesar Ceramiche facility in Florence, Italy, with imagery ©2022 Maxar Technologies, U.S. Geological Survey, USDA/FPAC/GEO. Map data ©2022.*

Plastic

Plastic production worldwide is steadily increasing. In 2018, global plastic production reached 359 million metric tons, 62 metric tons of which were produced in Europe. A main use of plastic in the Seattle house is in polyurethane insulation, which is derived from crude oil and natural gas.

ABS Pipe and PEX Pipe are made from resins and polyethylenes, through different manufacturers throughout the United States.

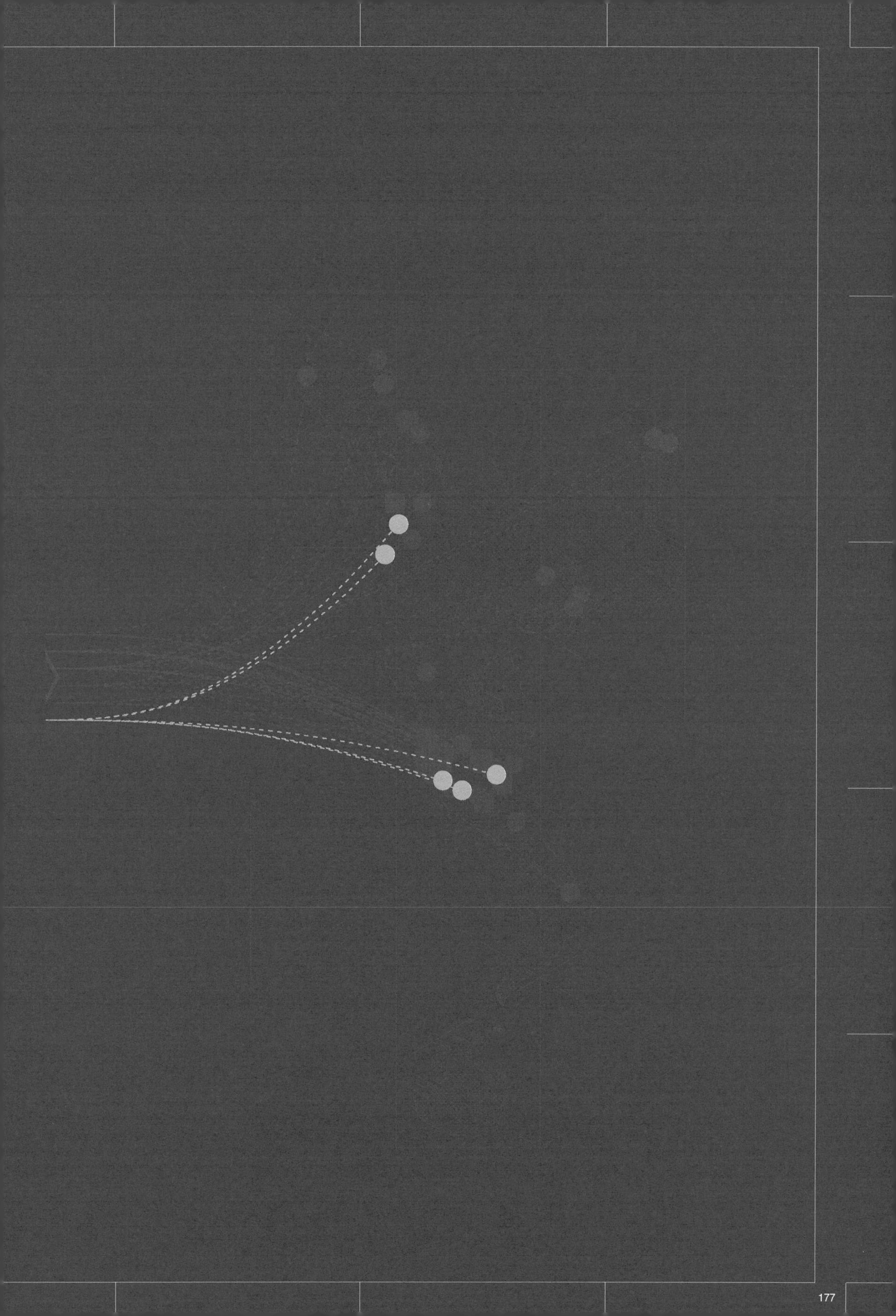

Crude Oil | Motiva

Crude oil is used to create polyurethane insulation used in the Seattle house.

The Motiva refinery is considered to be the largest oil refinery in the United States. In 1901 there was an oil boom in Texas that inspired the construction of a refinery in Port Arthur, TX. Operations began here in 1902.

Since then, Port Arthur's facility grew into Motiva Refinery and became the largest refinery in North America, with crude capacity of 630,000 barrels per day. This refinery takes up 1400 acres, employing 1500 people. Additionally, it also operates as the largest lubricant plant for consumers and commercial use.

+ *Motiva Oil Refinery in Port Arthur, TX, with imagery ©2022 Maxar Technologies, U.S. Geological Survey, USDA/FPAC/GEO. Map data ©2022.*

Natural Gas | Shell

Natural gas is used to create polyurethane insulation used in the Seattle house.

Natural gas can be used as a feedstock in the manufacturing process of many plastic products. The United States is the highest producer of natural gas, with around 32 billion MMcf per year.

Natural gas liquids, a key input for plastic production, are hard to transport. Petrochemical producers relying on natural gas liquids, or ethane, as a feedstock typically cluster geographically near sources of natural gas.

Shell facilities in Geismar, LA, with imagery ©2022 Maxar Technologies, U.S. Geological Survey, USDA/FPAC/GEO. Map data ©2022.

Polyurethane Insulation | BASF

Spraytite 158 Building Envelope Insulation is used as the material component of the Seattle house. This product is a two-component closed-cell spray polyurethane, manufactured by BASF SE.

BASF SE is the largest chemical company in the world. Founded in 1865, its headquarters are located in Ludwigshafen, Germany. Its facilities in Geismar, LA, and Wyandotte, MI, make its polyurethane products.

+ *BASF facilities in Geismar, LA, with imagery ©2022 Maxar Technologies, U.S. Geological Survey, USDA/FPAC/GEO. Map data ©2022.*

ABS Pipe | Charlotte Pipe & Foundry

Charlotte Pipe and Foundry was founded in 1901, but the plant did not start manufacturing plastic products until 1967. Its factories that produce ABS Pipe are located in North Carolina, Texas, Florida, Pennsylvania, Alabama, and Utah. It is likely the ABS Pipe for the house came from the Utah location, given its proximity to Seattle.

+ *Charlotte Pipe & Foundry in Utah, with imagery ©2022 Maxar Technologies, State of Utah, USDA/FPAC/GEO. Map data ©2022.*

Ethylene | Baystar

HDPE or high density polyethylene is used in the Seattle house, and is produced in tandem with ethylene cracking methods. Cracking breaks down the large molecules into smaller ones by application of high temperatures.

The production of ethylene is done through steam cracking of various hydrocarbons. In the United States, ethylene and propylene are produced from the cracking of ethane and propane, which makes the production cheaper and less complicated for operation.

The majority of ethylene in the United States is produced in Texas and Louisiana. One ethane and ethylene cracker built by Baystar in Port Arthur, TX, supplies the 625,00-ton-per-year polyethylene unit nearby.

Baystar facility with ethane cracker in Port Arthur, TX, with imagery ©2022 Houston-Galveston Area Council, Maxar Technologies, Texas General Land office, U.S. Geological Survey, USDA/FPAC/GEO. Map data ©2022.

PEX Pipe | RWC

PEX, or cross-linked polyethylene, is a water piping system that has been used in Europe since 1970 and in the United States since 1980. Since then, its use increased rapidly, replacing copper piping systems in many applications and forms. PEX pipe is produced by a few manufacturers, including RWC in Cullman, AL.

+ RWC facility in Cullman, AL, with imagery ©2022 Maxar Technologies, USDA/FPAC/GEO. Map data ©2022.

NEWS | ENVIRONMENT & HEALTH

Loopholes in Clean Air Act Are Letting a Texas Refinery Get Away With Pollution

Polyurethane and concrete admixtures are made near natural gas extraction points and oil refineries.

Production of plastic relies on natural gas and crude oil.

Fire Crews Respond To SE (

Thursday, April 14th 2022, 3:08 pm
By: News 9

Texas refinerie of tons of pollu

February 22, 2021 | 10:18 AM CST

Winds blow the smoke from a refinery i

HEALTH & SCIENCE

Small plant, big polluter

Thanks to a loophole in the Clean Air Act, William Koch's Oxbow plant in Arthur, Texas, puts out 10 times as much lung-damaging sulfur dioxide as industrial neighbors. People who live nearby have asked the state for hel avail.

SAVANNA STROTT, PUBLIC HEALTH WATCH / SAVANNA STROTT, PUBLIC HEALTH V LEFFLER, PUBLIC HEALTH WATCH
| NOVEMBER 2, 2021, 11:09 AM

Share

Evacuation orders in gas plant explosion

xplosion, Grass Fire

Port Arthur Residents Call For Civil Rights Probe Into How Texas Has Handled Air Pollution In Their Neighborhood

In a petition to the EPA, residents allege Texas has failed to adequately address sulfur dioxide emissions from the Oxbow Calcining plant, impacting the predominantly low income, black neighborhood.

KATIE WATKINS | AUGUST 18, 2021, 11:00 AM

Share

storm to hide release

ILKINS

as. Eric Gay | AP

Courtesy of Environmental Integrity Project

The Oxbow plant in Port Arthur at night.

due to concerns from ven

NEAR HAVEN

Fossil Fuels

Noxious Neighbors: The EPA Knows Tanks Holding Heavy Fuels Emit Harmful Chemicals. Why Are Americans Still at Risk?

The agency has been aware for more than a decade that companies are underreporting emissions, using equations developed by the petroleum industry that are often wrong.

ENVIRONMENT
Coalmont villagers fuming over black river
By Doris Maria Bregolisse · Global News
Posted August 27, 2013 6:59 pm · Updated August 27, 2013 9:34 pm
Coal slurry escapes from containment pond, turns Tulameen river black
By justinmcelroyglobalnews · Global News
Posted August 26, 2013 9:30 pm · Updated August 26, 2013 9:42 pm
-A A+
Approximately 6,000 gallons of coal tailings from Coalmont Energy spilled
Monitoring reveals Indonesia's 'legal timber' scheme riddled with violations
by Hans Nicholas Jong on 29 September 2021
Illegal mangrove logging surges in Indonesia's Batam amid economic hardship
by Yogi Eka Sahputra on 10 December 2021 | Translated by Basten Gokkon

Death metal: tin mining in Indonesia

If you own a mobile, it's probably held together by tin from the Indonesian island of Bangka. Mining is wrecking the

year it claims dozens more lives

in from the sea in Indonesia

s on land in Indonesia continue to twindle, miners are

sea.

Tin oxide is used in glass.

Coking coal is used in steel production.

Timber and wood from Indonesia is used in the house's plywood.

Photograph: Ulet Ifansasti/Friends Of The Earth

a mobile phone, so he uses a friend's to tell us the

want any visitors and he won't talk. ~~His boss has~~

ay anything. They're neighbours and the mine's

and he needs this job - the job he hopes to go back

hallah - because mining is good money.

ase don't come.

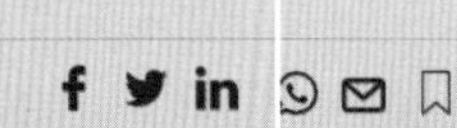

Tin mines close in on an Indonesian hamlet still clinging to nature

by Taufik Wijaya on 16 June 2021 | Adapted by Intan Iskandar

wooden p

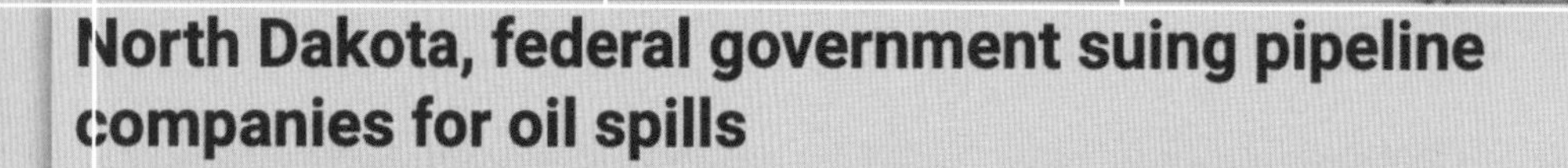

North Dakota, federal government suing pipeline companies for oil spills

The production of plastic relies on natural gas and crude oil.

Stone quarries supply tile for the house.

Concrete aggregate yards cause air pollution.

Going beyond the lim
develops novel expos
statistical methods fo
oil spill study

Tuesday, April 12, 2022

FROM THE EXPERTS

Deepwater Horizon Oil Spill Anniversary Is a Grave Reminder of Why Not to Trust the Oil Industry

APRIL 20, 2022

BY
SAMBHAV SANKAR

The only thing we can truly trust this industry to do is fight to preserve its business model and secure profits for its

Fire boat response crews battle the blazing remnants of the offshore oil rig Deepwater Horizon.

rizon oil spill involved over 9,
, Louisiana and Mississippi a
/NIEHS)

The Danger and Allure of Italy's 'White Gold'

Amid a Boom in Mosque Construction, Builders Turn to Italy's 'White Gold'

EMBED SHARE

J researcher
sessment
water Horizon

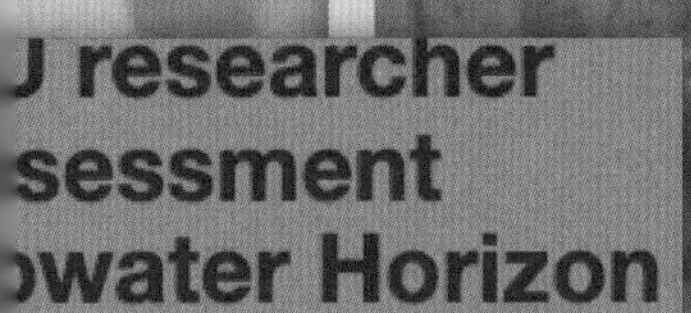

yed in the Gulf of Mexico waters
nds of workers on the water and

urers killed in marble mine slide in KP's Buner

blished February 22, 2020

ork at the site of the mine collapse. — Photo by author

Concrete Dust Blowing Into Butchertown Neighborhood For Decades

By Ryan Van Velzer

Labors

Labors

Labors

Labor consciousness—multi-layered and global in reach

Even a small building like the Seattle house compels a huge number of human and non-human bodies into action. The composition and embodied energy of the house is as much its material as it is its labor. Behind every material there are several processes. And behind every process, there are bodies.

Labor. Workers. Legal. Illegal. Human and non-human.

Here we show that the work undertaken to build a house consists of much more than just the architect and consultants sitting behind their desks at an office and the construction workers at the site. Labor begins long before the architect draws the first line—it begins with the extraction of the raw materials used to manufacture the products that will eventually create the house. Most of this occurs long before the building is even a project on the architect's table; such as are the timelines of the supply chains. Specialist labor practices take over the transportation and manufacturing processes required to transform raw ingredients into the finished product. Eventually, the architect enters the timeline, funnelling the labor output of thousands into a design—in this case a single-family house. The labor of architectural design takes many months, and the product of this labor is less physical than that of the labor processes that come before and after the architect.

Non-human labors, such as the work of the micro-biomes that breakdown wood, are little understood in the building industry - they require a book of their own.

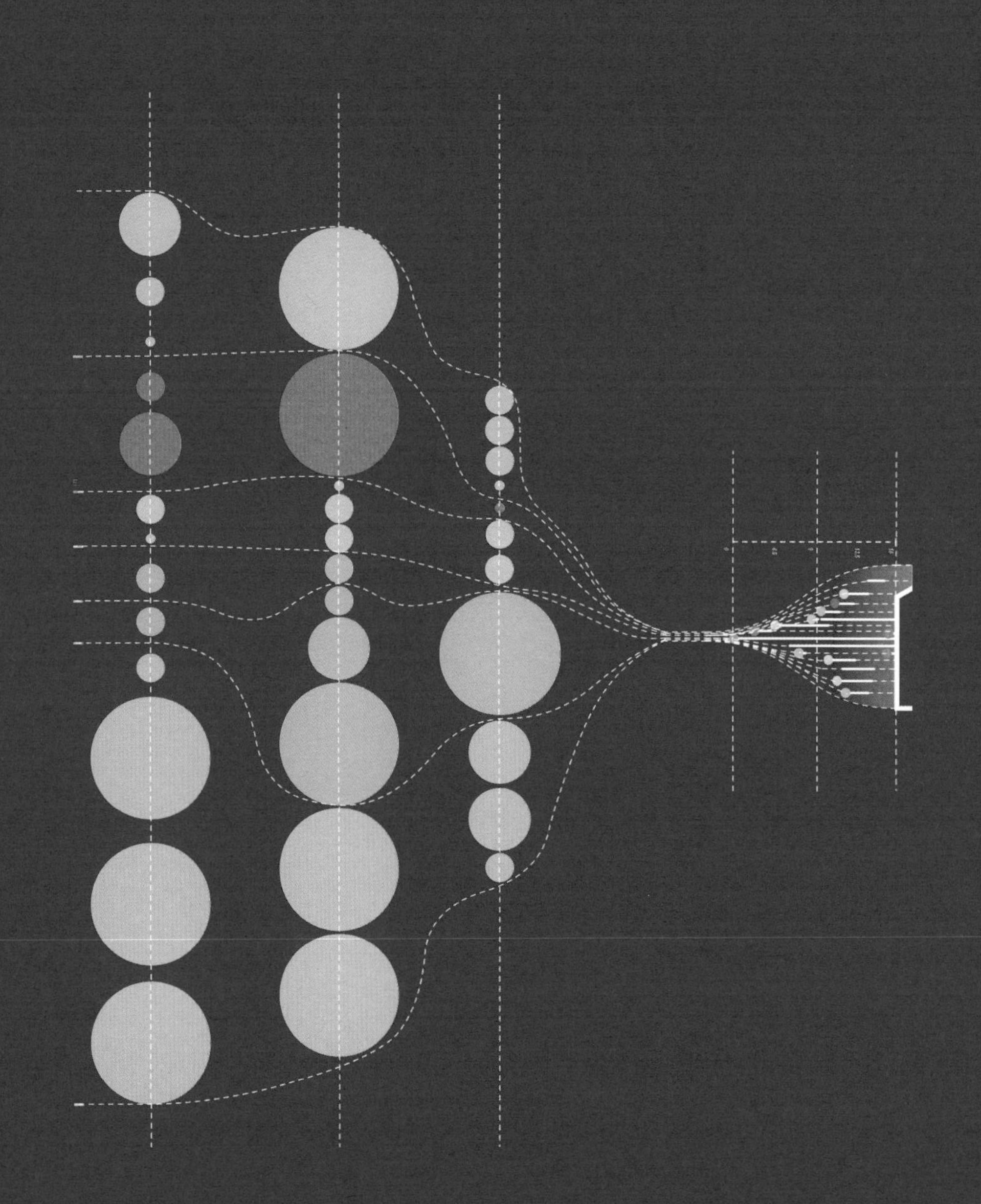

Jason W. Moore teaches world ecology at Binghamton University, where he is professor of sociology. He is the author or editor of Capitalism in the Web of Life: Ecology and the Accumulation of Capital *(Verso, 2015) and* A History of the World in Seven Cheap Things: A Guide to Capitalism, Nature, and the Future of the Planet *(University of California Press, 2017) with Raj Patel.*

"Capitalism makes nature and the web of life makes capitalism."

"Capitalism works, not because it does terrible things to natures (it does), but because it has been successful at mobilising and appropriating manifold natures for free or low cost."

"Cheap Nature has never been a bargain. Cheapness is violence; it grows from the barrel of a gun. It's an utterly irrational system of rationality, one premised on mobilising the work of all natures—humans included—for free, or for as close to free as possible. That's crucial because capitalism is everything that an efficient system is not. Capitalism's prodigious waste of life and limb is fundamental to its logic."

"How do the practical matters of domination facilitate the practical matters of exploitation, and vice versa?"

Sourcing / Extraction

Long before the house is even a project with a budget line for the client, the labors that will ultimately result in the making of the house are already at work, feeding the supply chains of the construction industry. It is almost impossible to draw a line that can connect a specific early stage labor used in extraction to a specifc material used in the construction of the house.

This is well beyond the concept of the alienation of labor as theorized by the 19th century Marxist, even though the roots of the process are traceable back to the global colonial extraction processes of that time. Our contemporary global supply chains have created a new era of alienated labors, atomized beyond retrieval. Even so, almost all construction around the world, depends on it. Even a small chink in the supply chain can result in a global economic crisis, as we experienced during the Covid 19 shutdowns. This makes the everydays of our daily life vulnerable to an unknowable globally extractive world.

At a local level, this means that it is well neigh impossible to be sure that all that we build with, and consume, has never been processed via exploitative labor practices. Directly and indirectly, all human lives, via their labors, are interconnected, interdependent and, perhaps most importantly, inter-responsible to each other.

Although nearly impossible to understand or diagram, this kind of inter-responsible accounting, (which is also an accounting of our inter-ir-responsibility), especially when indexed to climate change, is THE ethical imperative of our times.

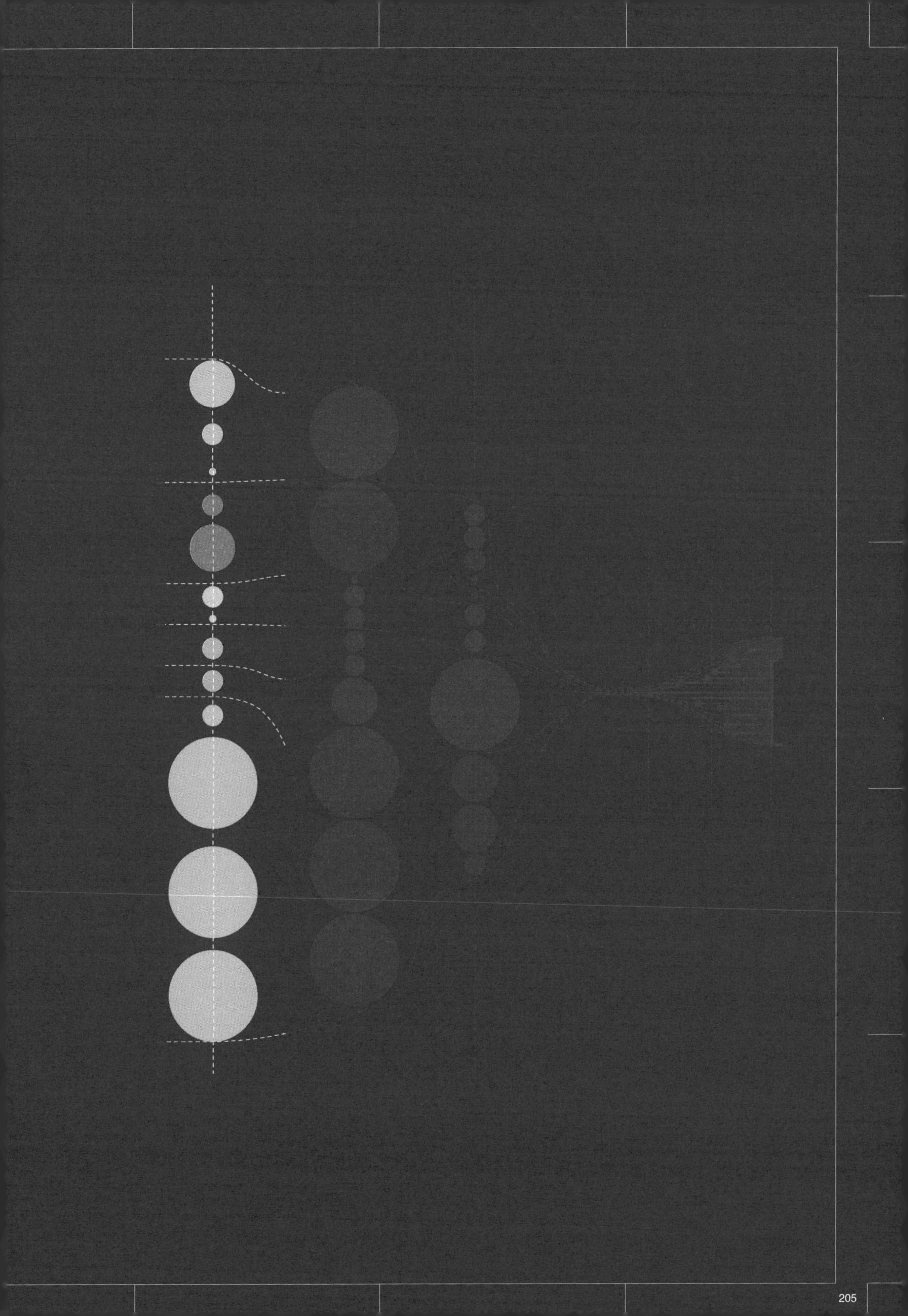

Manufacturing

The manufacturing phase of the labor story is quite opaque. We know that after the raw materials have been extracted from the earth, they are transported to manufacturing plants to be processed into finished goods. The labor behind these processes is extremely varied and is scattered across skill and education levels. It takes on a variety of appearances, from laboratory research, to robotic operation, to heavy lifting. How many different kinds of labor does it take for a material to go from raw substance to final product? How many laborers are at each stage of the process? What are their stories?

Manufacturing labor covers such a broad range of work that these oftentimes grimy stories from the past remain - are kept? - obscured in a field as aesthetics and future use oriented as architecture. This is not just a question of "lean-construction" and ensuring that the manufacturers and fabricators are at the same table with the architects and construction managers. This is not about further optimization of the supply chains via digitization and minimization of waste and delays.

Rather it is about taking cognizance of the fact that simple, pure lines and blank facades of a modern architecture derived aesthetic sensibility and ethical claim are today completely out of sync with the profound complexities of the global manufacturing supply chains. If form were to follow supply chain, contemporary architecture could not be about the "machine-aesthetic," i.e. about standardization, optimization, transparency, and such; it would have to be about mysterious origins, obscured labors and indecipherable sources. It would have be, in other words, about magic.

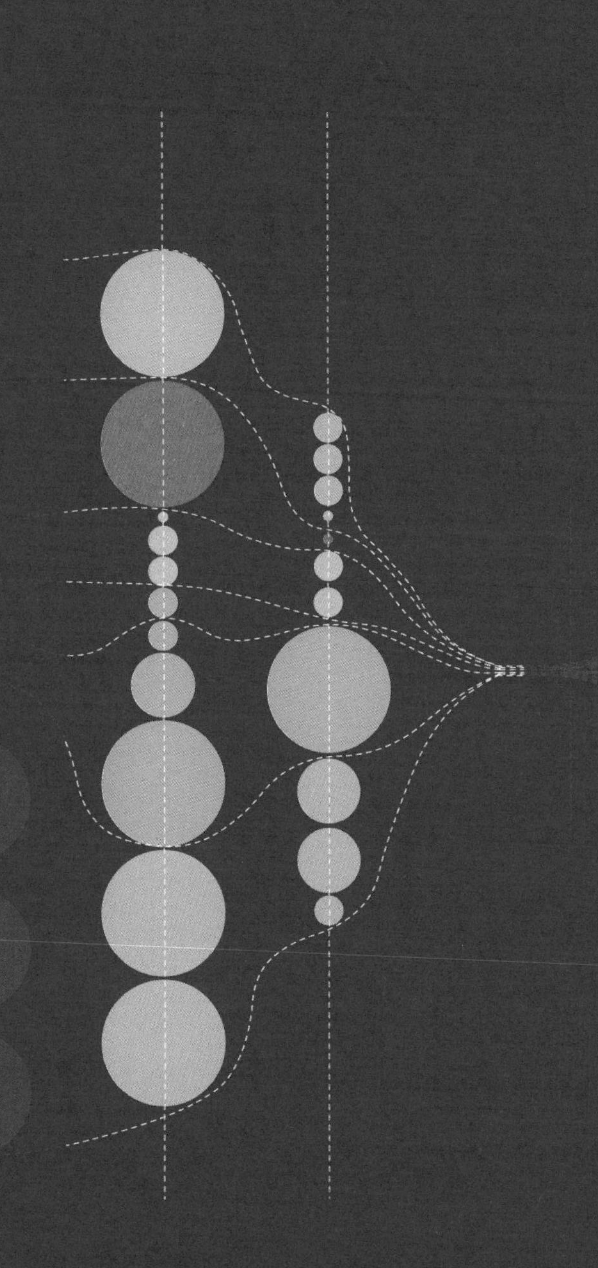

Design / Construction

We now enter the final (and perhaps most known) phase of the human labor story: design and construction. This is where the house's "architects" arrives on the scene, with their retinue of contractors, sub-contractors, fabricators and consultants. In thirteen months, the house went from design to completion. Here, you can see that the architects and contractor were the first people to enter the story. For the initial six months, these two entities worked hand in hand, trying to find the right fabricators and laborers for the job. Construction administration is usually, but not always, within the expected services of the architects.

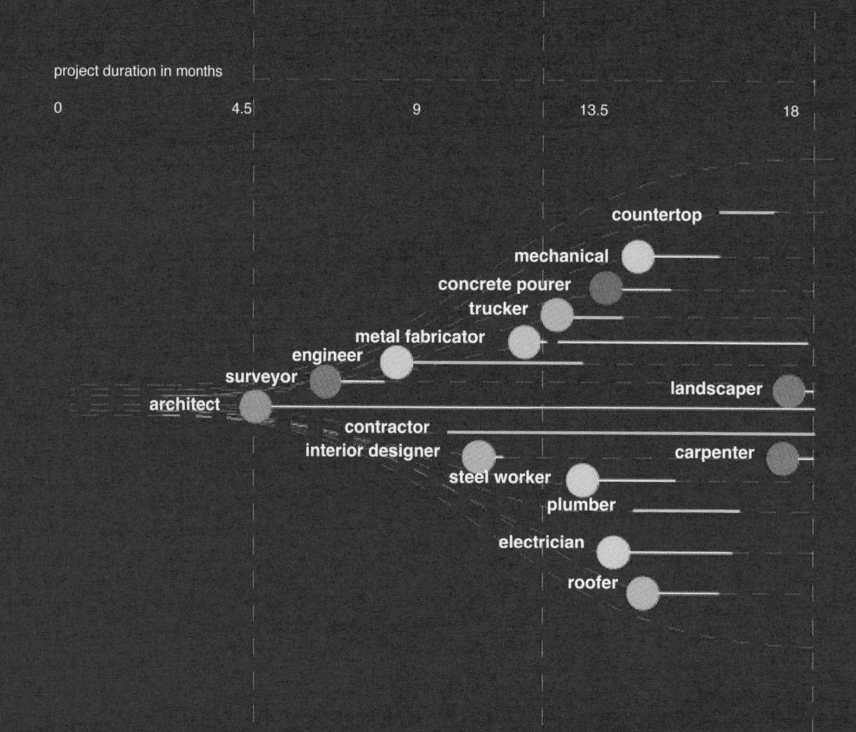

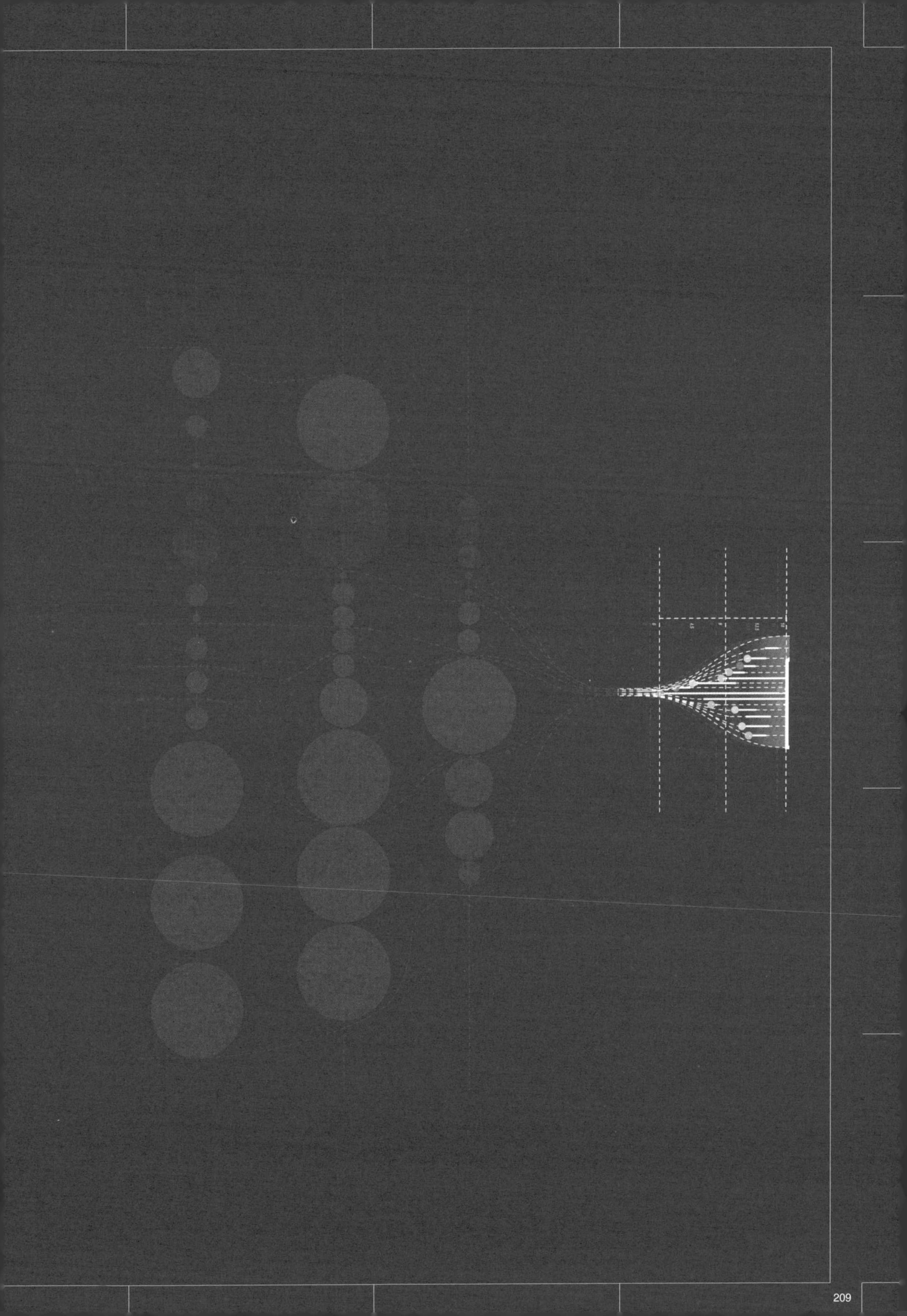

Design represents the total work that was conducted prior to construction, and in the Seattle house case consumed 18% of the total number of hours worked. While architects are generally thought of as the most significant players, there are many other people involved that begin to have influence over the project long before construction has started. For example, surveyors analyze the site's topography, and the geotech inspector assesses soil integrity. During this time, the architects were continuously working on drawings and details, obtaining permits from the city of Seattle, and working towards a finished design that could eventually be built to the clients' satisfaction.

Contemporary design practices, particularly small ones like Allied8, usually aspire to source their products ethically and as locally and sustainably as possible. Allied8 identified ethical sourcing and labor practices as central to thier mission. But, this is a complex juggling act that requires balancing availability of information with billable-hours spent with the aesthetic and fiscal expectations of the client. Most fall short, due to the exigencies of the process, satisfied to have at least "made a difference".

Design work, in this sense, given the limitations of its scope as compared with the size of its ambitions, suffers from the same delimna faced by the practices of daily life as, for instance, promoted by the slogan "Think global, act local." How is one actually to do that given the opacity of the global? Is it good enough to just compost one's coffee beans and say: "Well, I did something"?

\+ *The design teams, including Strong Work Structural Engineers, Allied8 architects, and Anne Viggiano Color & Design.*

STRONG WORK
STRUCTURAL ENGINEERING

HOME SERVICES PROJECTS ABOUT BLOG RESOURCES CONTACT

PROFILE

Michael Chamberlain, SE, LEED AP, CSBA

Senior Structural Engineer

Michael Chamberlain has over 20 years of Structural Engineering and Construction Administration experience. Since 1995, Michael has created structural solutions for over 800 buildings and homes in the greater Seattle area. Michael's experience includes structural systems constructed of concrete, steel, wood, masonry and aluminum.

Michael has a passion for creating a collaborative environment, and prioritizes responsiveness to his clients, architects, and contractors. Only through dialogue, not just the calculator, can we produce the most cost-effective, buildable structural solutions.

- **1996:** Michael achieved a Bachelors of Science in Civil Engineering and a Bachelor of the Arts in the Humanities at Seattle University, graduating Magna Cum Laude.
- **2002:** Michael achieved his Professional Engineer license, passing an eight hour exam.
- **2004:** Michael achieved his Structural Engineer license, passing two eight-hour exams.
- **2007:** Michael graduated from University of Washington with his Masters in Civil Engineering while continuing to work professionally as a Structural Engineer.
- **2008:** Michael became certified as a LEED Accredited Professional.
- **2009:** Michael founded his own company: Strong Work Structural Engineering.
- **2010:** Michael completed a nine-month course, achieving certification as a Sustainable Building Advisor.

WORK **STUDIO** NEWS PRESS CONTACT allied8

Allied8 Team

Barbara Busetti
Architect, Partner
b@allied8.com
resume

Leah Martin
Architect, Partner
leah@allied8.com
resume

Stefan Schwarzkopf
Architect, Partner
stefan@allied8.com
resume

Matias Bervejillo
Architectural Designer
matias@allied8.com

Jessica Aceves
Office Administartor, Architectural Drafter
jessica@allied8.com

Hannah Kramer
Architectural Designer
hannah@allied8.com

Color & Design Studio

Anne Viggiano

Suzy Scott

Lyndsey Bosko

Liz Brayer

Dan Kopsak

Fiona Kelly

Collaborators

Allied8 Architects

Molly Andrews Burke of Chairloom

3D printing using concrete could displace labor on construction sites.

Top 10 Largest Steel Producing Companies in the World

There are quite a large number of steel manufacturers in the steel industry, who become more popular by producing steel in large quantities.

Here is the list of top 10 largest steel producing companies in the world.

1. ArcelorMittal
ArcelorMittal, who operates in more than 60 countries, is headquartered in Avenue de la Liberte, Luxembourg. It was formed in 2006 by the merger of Arcelor and Mittal Steel. The company has 232,000 employees and it produces

construc

(Kazakhs

Architects: Here's the Problem With 3D-Printed Buildings

It's still not clear if this technology is going to save the world or be another decorative footnote of architectural history.

Jack Balderrama Morley

DETAILS

OPINION

The Oak Ridge National Laboratory, the same place that developed the atomic bomb, recently produced a little white structure with a vehicle attached that it says demonstrates the future of construction. Both the structure and vehicle are 3D-printed, produced via enlarged versions of the same tabletop machines that have become popular with "makers" around the world. Building-scale printers work the same way as their smaller cousins, depositing thin layers of material over previous

Construction Robots Will Change the Industry Forever

Robotics Online Marketing Team | 04/17/2018

The construction industry is one of the least automated industries that feature manual-intensive labor as a primary source of productivity. Whether it's new commercial construction, renovation or demolition, robots don't yet play a significant role in any step of a building's lifecycle.

There are several new robots under development and in the early stages of deployment that could change this, however. As a highly unautomated industry, construction is poised for a robot revolution.

Why Are Construction Robots Only Now Realizing Commercial Potential?

It may seem odd that the construction industry utilizes so few robots, but there's a good reason for this: construction tasks are notoriously difficult to automate. The construction worksite is the primary obstacle

TIME

SUBSCRIBE

ow the Company Behind TikTok's Viral 3D-Printed Houses Wants to Help Solve the Affordable Housing Crisis

Labor protections in design and construction vary by role, employer, and jurisdiction.

Construction worker suing Microsoft, Skanska, Balfour Beatty for racial discrimination

Bargaining for Be

Unioniz stalled movem

By Sydney Franklir
Practice

The Woolworth Builc
Mobili/Via Wikimedi

Construction trades celebrating return of concrete workers

VIDEO: Constructions trades cel

Seattle concrete mixers, truck drivers offer to return to work while strike negotiations continue

—

The months-long strike has stalled many major construction projects around Seattle, like the West Seattle Bridge and a new UW psychiatric hospital.

Sea dri stri

—

The m
aroun
hospit

Architects Are the Latest White-Collar Workers to Confront Bosses

they are overworked and underpaid, architects at a prominent
rk firm want to unionize. Others could follow.

this article 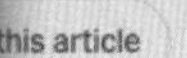   199

led their

at SHoP Architects
it architecture's labor
far from over

022 • Architecture, East, Editor's Picks, News, Professional

attan, where SHoP Architects is headqu
ssed under CC BY-SA 2.0)

Architecture union launches to fight 'toxic culture' of overwork

30 OCTOBER 2019 . BY ELLA JESSEL

Architecture workers have formed the a new trade union to combat what it describes as the sector's 'toxic culture' of overwork, underpay and discrimination

America desperately needs 1 million more construction workers

By Vanessa Yurkevich, CNN Business

Updated 6:36 PM ET, Sun July 11, 2021

concret
ffer to
gotiati

strike has st
ke the West

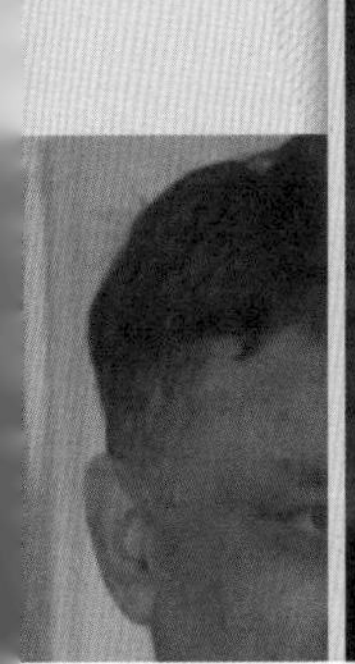

Atoms

Atoms

Atoms

Atomic consciousness—
the ultimate character of all things, our connectedness to the life and time cycles of our planet, our solar system, and our Universe.

Long before compounds are manufactured into things usable by the humans, all the atoms and their associated compounds were manufactured in three places:

ON THE PHOTOSYNTHETIC SURFACE OF THE EARTH (BOTANY):

The first land plants appeared around 470 million years ago. This is the source of the various rubbers, but also of the woods, even though all the woods were 'grown' within the last century and a half.

(0–150 years: 470 million years ago)

ON EARTH (BIO-GEOLOGY):

This is the source of various compounds created through heat and compression: such as magnesium ore, silicone, and oil. Most of the components of steel, glass, and concrete were created within this time-space continuum.

(0–4.5 billion years ago)

IN THE UNIVERSE (ASTROPHYSICS):

The Big Bang was 13.7 billion years ago. Some of the metal in the house may have been formed a billion years later with the first super nova explosions. Most of the metals, however, were likely formed in the supernovas that just preceded the formation of the solar system 4.5 billion years ago. All steel, indeed all heavy metal, carries with it the memory of a supernova explosion somewhere in the universe.

(4.5 billion to 12 billion years ago)

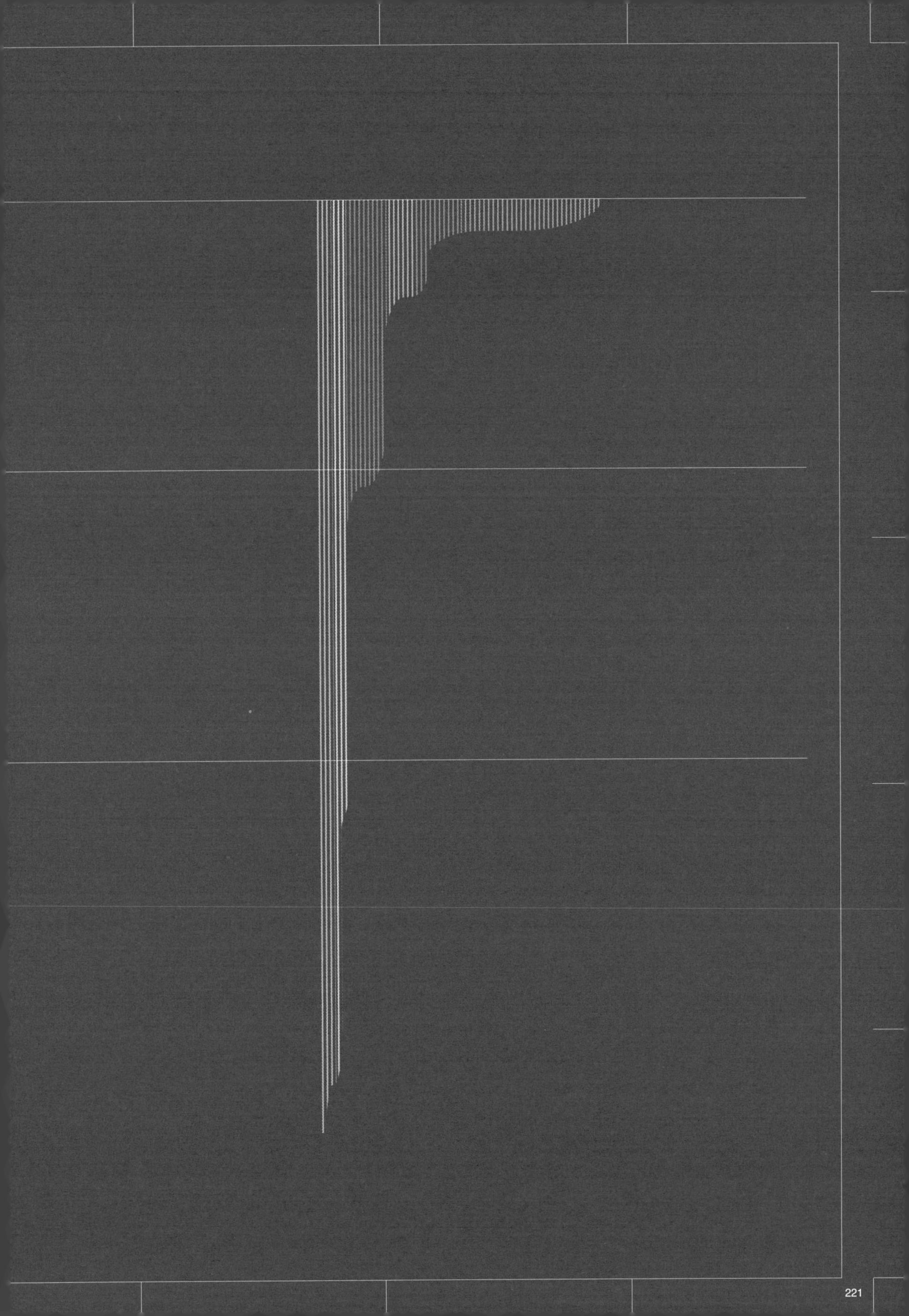

Karen Barad *Meeting the Universe Halfway: Quantum Physics and the Entanglement of Matter and Meaning (Durham, NC: Duke University Press, 2007).*

Karen Barad's theory of agential realism holds that the universe comprises phenomena, which are "the ontological inseparability of intra-acting agencies." By this formulation, architecture cannot be distinguished between human and non-human actors, "organic" material (like wood) and "inorganic material (like metal), and such. Intra-action makes the ontology of architecture indistinguishable from, and constitutively entangled with, its epistemology. Architecture, the building and the design, are both "material-discursive" phenomenon.

Barad takes her inspiration from physicist Niels Bohr, one of the founders of quantum physics. Because specific practices of mattering have ethical consequences, excluding other kinds of mattering, onto-epistemological practices are always in turn onto-ethico-epistemological. Per Barad, material practices have an an innate ethical property that cannot be sliced apart from their materiality.

"Eros, desire, life forces run through everything, not only specific body parts or specific kind of engagements among body parts. Matter itself is not a substrate or a medium for the flow of desire...Matter feels, converses, suffers, desires, yearns and remembers."

- Karen Barad.

Photosynthesis

Photosynthesis on the surface of the earth is thought to have started 3.4 billion years ago and is responsible for providing the planet's atmosphere with most of its oxygen. Geological evidence suggests that photosynthesis in cyanobacteria exploded 2.4 billion years ago, during a period referred to as the "Oxygen Catastrophe." This name is a tribute to the extinction of most existing species on Earth, which did not survive such a surge in oxygen content.

Indeed, if oxygen is necessary for complex life as we know it today, such an increase of biologically produced molecular oxygen (dioxygen, O_2) changed Earth's atmosphere from a weakly reducing atmosphere to an oxidizing atmosphere, causing many or most existing species on Earth to die out.

Despite that, cyanobacteria responsible for the productions of this oxygen are often credited with having allowed for the development of multicellular forms and the life diversity we know today.

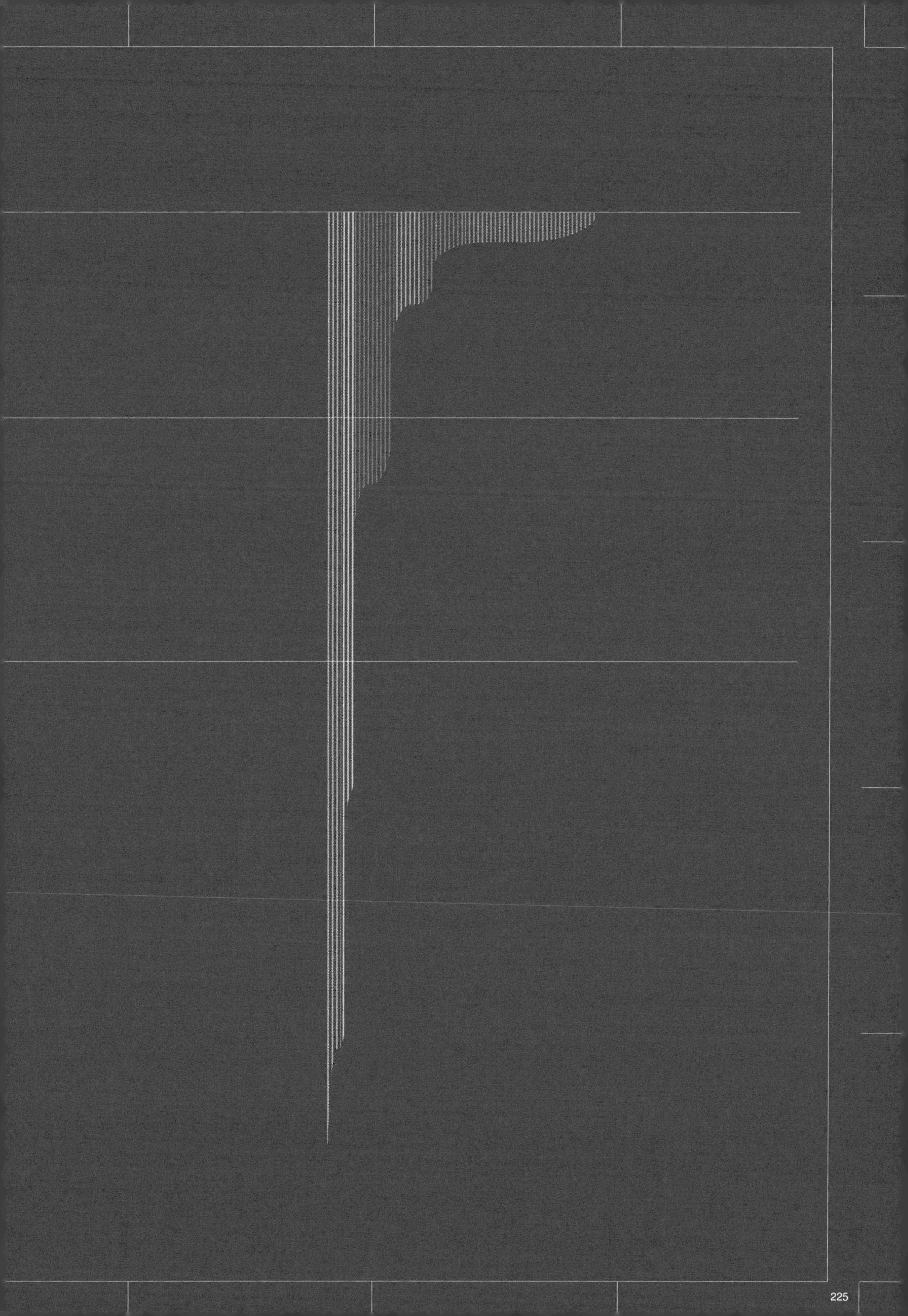

Geology

CHEMICAL AND ORE HORIZON: The earth is 4.543 billion years old. In its early volcanic phase, the metals that originated from outer space fused with silicone and other minerals to form complex ores. More than 80% of the Earth's surface—above and below sea level—is of volcanic origin. The oceanic conditions for limestone, by contrast, developed "only" 350 million years ago.

PLANT HORIZON: The first land plants appeared around 470 million years ago, during the Ordovician period, when life was diversifying rapidly. They were non-vascular plants, like mosses and liverworts. Grasses developed only around 55 million years ago. The conditions that would eventually create coal began to develop about 300 million years ago.

OIL HORIZON: The formation of oil takes a significant amount of time. It first appeared 252 million years ago, though most appeared later closer to 66 million years ago.

TREE HORIZON: The earliest known tree-like plants are the Gilboa trees (*Eospermatopteris*). They date back 385 million years ago. Oaks first appear about 32–35 million years ago

SAND HORIZON: Sands are basically produced through the friction of rock against rock and so is very recent as far as Earth sciences go. Stone takes time to decompose, especially quartz (silica) and feldspar. Often starting thousands of miles from the ocean, rocks travel slowly along rivers and streams, constantly breaking down en route. Some sand is composed of shells, coral skeletons, and other biological precipitates. Most sand dates betwee 5 million to 12,000 years old.

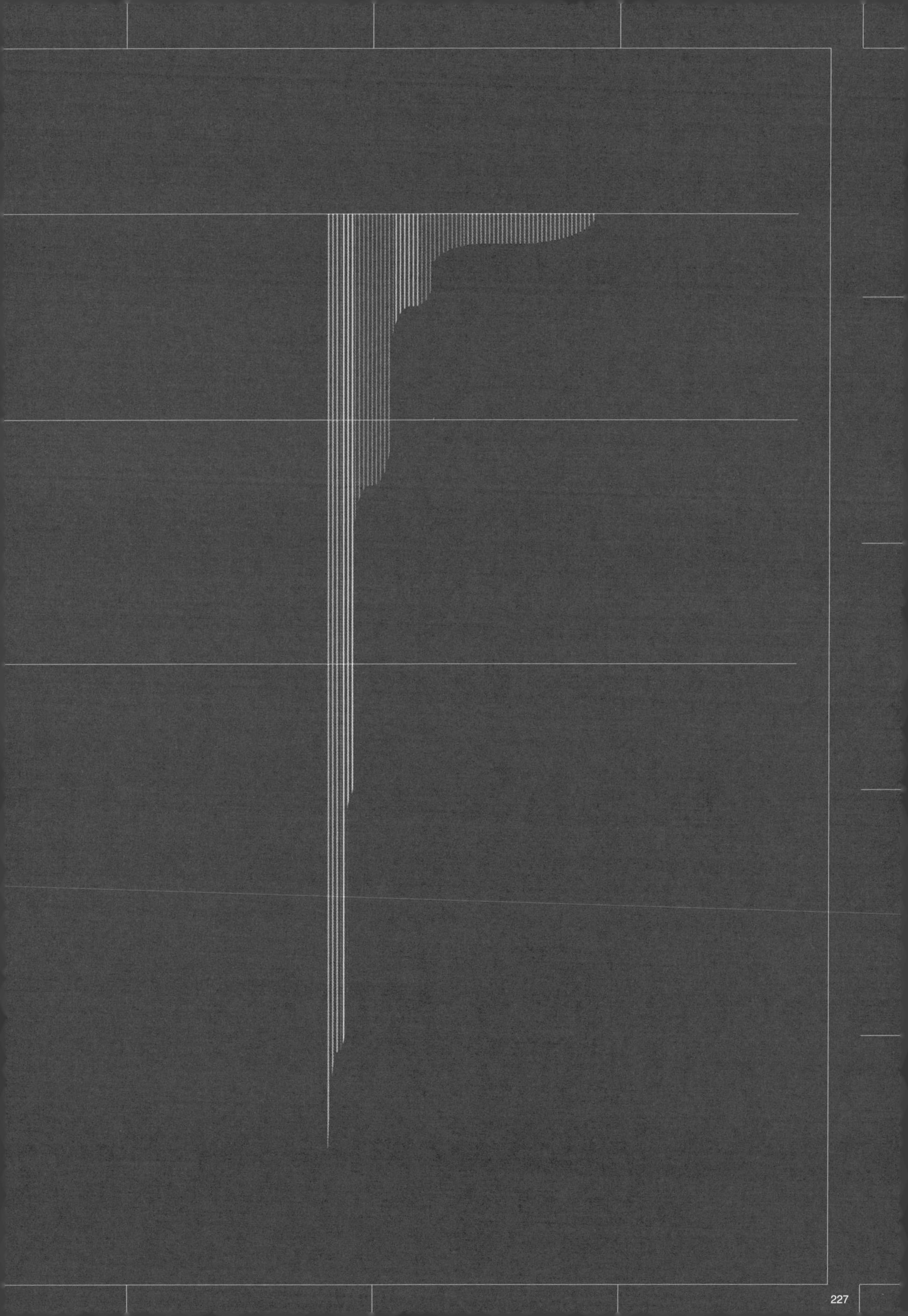

Chemical / Ore Horizon: Limestone

Limestone

Bingham Canyon Mine, located just southwest of Salt Lake City, UT, is one of the largest open-pit mines in the world. The Kennecott Utah Copper Company removes about half a million tons of material from the mine every day.

The majority of porphyry deposits are Phanerozoic in age, i.e. from our current gelogic eon with abundant animal and plant life. It began about 538 million years ago.

Limestone mines produce several different products used in the production of both concrete and glass.

+ *A limestone quarry near Orosei on Sardinia, Italy, in a photo by Michael J. Zirbes (Wikimedia Commons).*

+ *Extraction work at a limestone quarry in Minya, Egypt, in a photo by Mgalal20 (Wikimedia Commons).*

+ *Pouring concrete in Trimingham, Norfolk, United Kingdom, in a photo by Kolforn (Wikimedia Commons).*

Porphyry Copper Deposits

Bingham Canyon Mine is one of the largest open-pit mines in the world, located just southwest of Salt Lake City, UT. The Kennecott Utah Copper Company removes about half a million tons of material from the mine every day.

The majority of porphyry deposits are Phanerozoic in age, or from 538.8 million years ago to the present.

Copper is used in the house in pipes.

+ *The Bingham Canyon Mine as seen in a photo by Steven Vance (Flicker).*

+ *Copper from a mine in North Carolina, United States, in a photo by Robert M. Lavinsky (Wikimedia Commons).*

+ *Copper connections in the basement of the Seattle house in a photo by Vikramaditya Prakash.*

Trona Ore

Trona is mined as the primary source of sodium carbonate, or soda, in the United States. Soda is used as a flux element in making glass for glass windows.

In Wyoming, where the soda used in the house was likely mined, the trona deposits were made during the Paleogene period, 66 million to 23 million years ago.

+ *The Trona Pinnacles, located in California, in a photo by Bobak Ha'Eri (Wikimedia Commons).*

+ *Trona ore in a photo by Andrew Silver (Wikimedia Commons).*

+ *Air and water pressure testing for windows in the Seattle house in a photo by Vikramaditya Prakash.*

Magnesite

Magnesite occurs as veins in rock types, such as dolomite. It can appear in deposits that date to the Neogene period, which spans the end of the Paleogene period 23.03 million years ago to the beginning of the present Quaternary period 2.58 million years ago.

Magnesite is burnt to make magnesium oxide. Magnesium oxide is used in ceramics, in Portland cement mix, and as a stabilizer in glass production.

+ *A magnesite mine in a photo by HariHaran771981 (Wikimedia Commons).*

+ *Magnesite in Salem, Tamil Nardu, India, in a photo by ShiluGeo1PU (Wikimedia Commons).*

+ *Blue Circle Southern Cement factory in New South Wales, Australia, in a photo by AYArktos (Wikimedia Commons).*

Oil Horizon

Crude oil is a fossil fuel, that is formed from the dead bodies of organic life, in particular plants and tiny marine animals. Over hundreds of milllons of years, organic mateiral collected at the bottom of oceans, riverbeds and swamps and such, is subjected to heat and pressure transforming it into petroleum or natural gas.

Coal

The same process of heat and pressure when subjected to dead wood produces coal. Around 90% of all coal beds were deposited during just 2% of the earth's geologic history, 360 to 260 million years ago.

Coal ash is used in concrete mix, and petroleum products are used to make plastics. Coal is still used as an energy source in some places for manufacturing.

\+ *A coal mine near Hailar, Inner Mongolia, in a photo by Henry Lawford (Flicker).*

\+ *The interior of the Yacimientos Carboníferos Río Turbio Coal Mine in a photo by the Agencia Popular de Comunicación Suramericana (Wikimedia Commons).*

Big Bang / Nucleosynthesis

In the early life of the universe, the only atoms present were hydrogen, helium, and lithium. This minority of elements lasted until about 400,000 years after the Big Bang when radiation was too high for atoms to stabilize. At that point the three elements produced high-mass stars that burnt bright consuming their fuel fast, going supernova in just a few million years. Their intense heat ionized the particles around them, and produced the first set of heavier metals in the supernova process. Subsequent generations of stars “refined” these metals and enriched them producing the 118 known elements of our current periodic table. This is called nucleosynthesis.

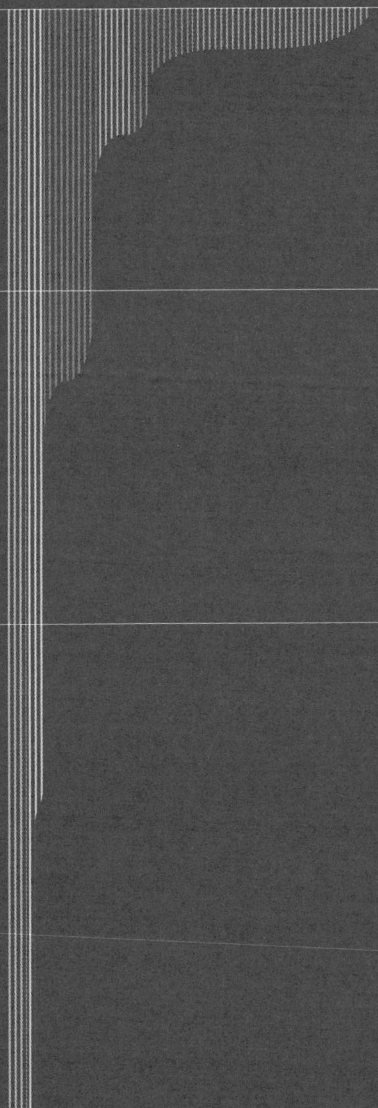

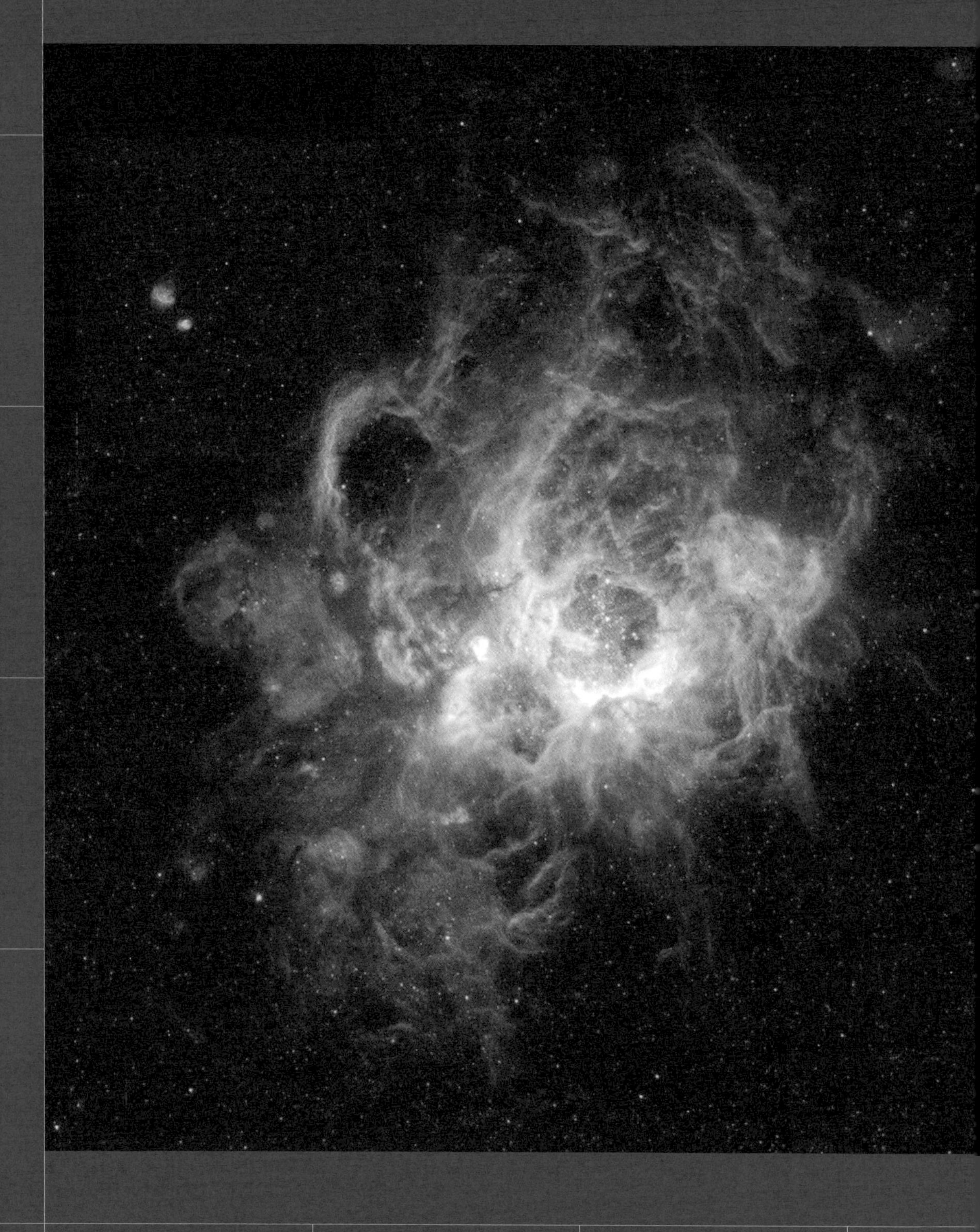

“The cosmos is within us. We are made of star-stuff. We are a way for the universe to know itself.”

— Carl Sagan

“Consciousness is evolution’s solution to dealing with big data.”

— Memo Akten

NGC 604, a giant region of ionized hydrogen in the Triangulum Galaxy, in a photo by NASA from the Hubble Space Telescope (Wikimedia Commons).

Our solar system's known elements—other than hydrogen, helium, and lithium—were made through nucleosynthesis after the Big Bang.

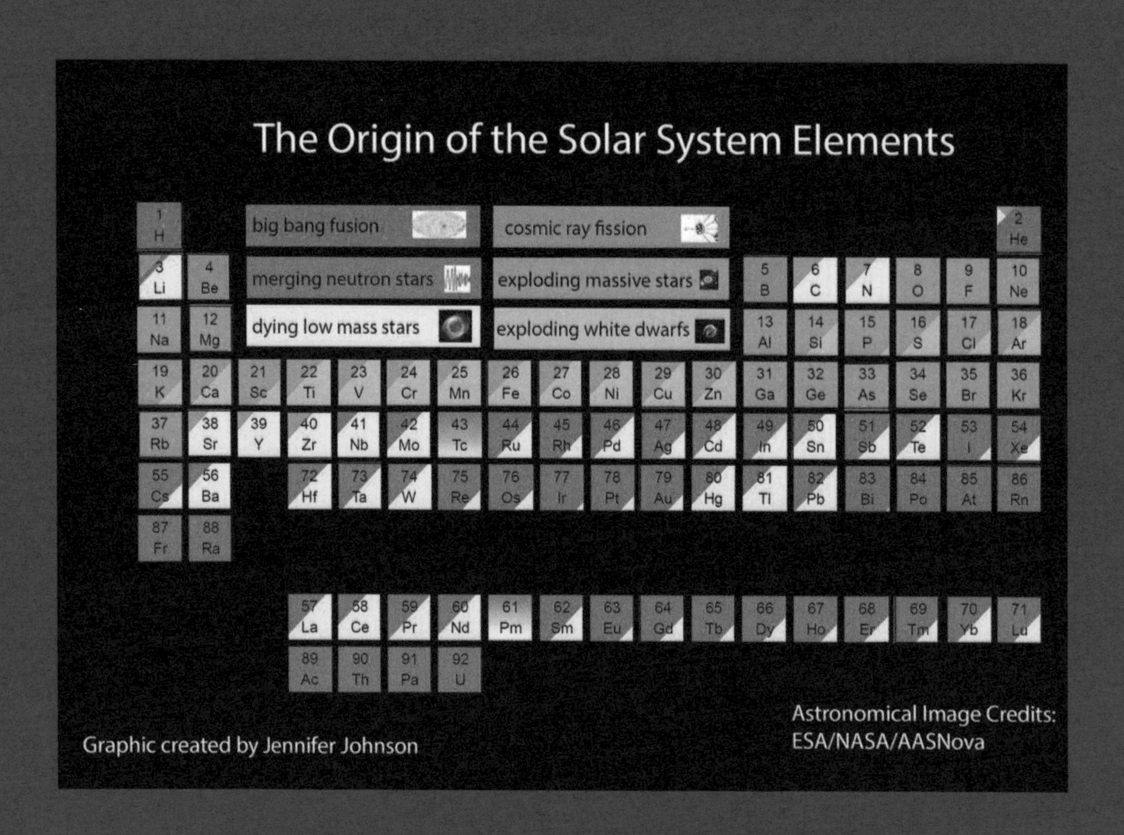

+ The Origin of the Solar System Elements *by Jennifer Johnson (Wikimedia Commons).*

Stellar nucleosynthesis or nucleo-enrichment took place over the universe's 14 billion years at varying rates and forms producing the "metals" we currently know. Merging neutron stars, i.e. stars made only on neutrons, and dying low mass stars account for most of the heaviest metals in the universe.

Our solar system's known elements—other than hydrogen, helium, and lithium—were made through nucleosynthesis after the Big Bang.

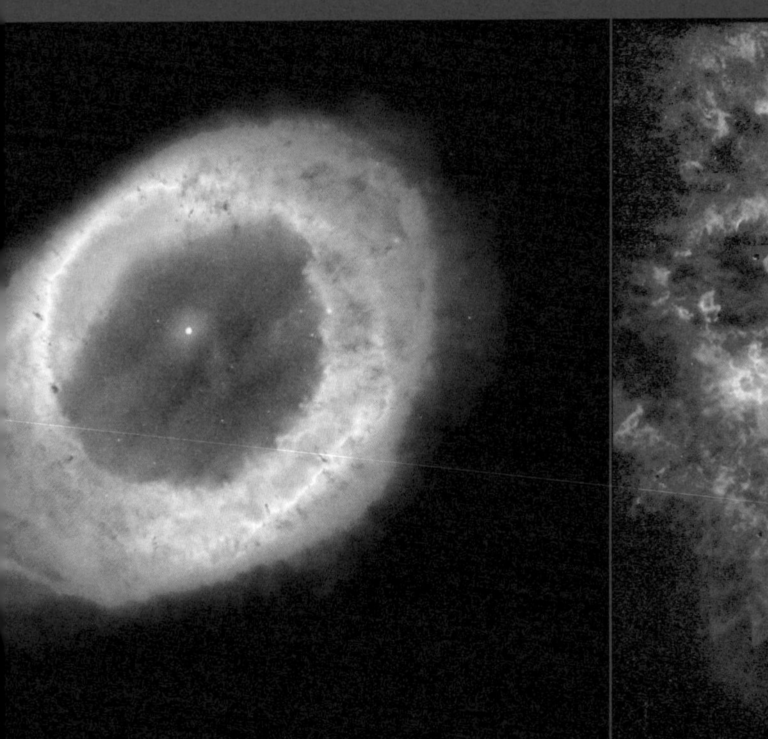

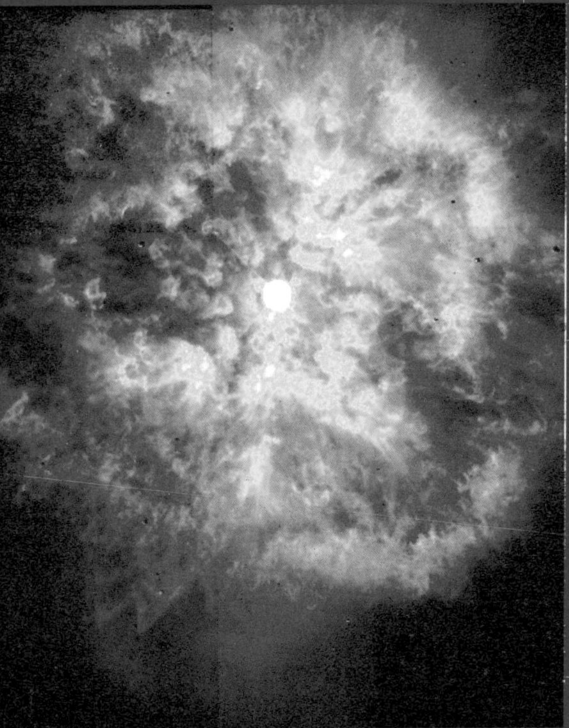

+ *An exploding star scattering heavy metals into space in a photo by Pablo Carlos Budassi (Wikimedia Commons).*

+ *WR124 exploding in a photo by NASA from the Hubble Space Telescope (Wikimedia Commons).*

Elements created from merging neutron stars and dying low mass stars include radium, tungsten, silver, tin, mercury, gold, platinum, and lead.

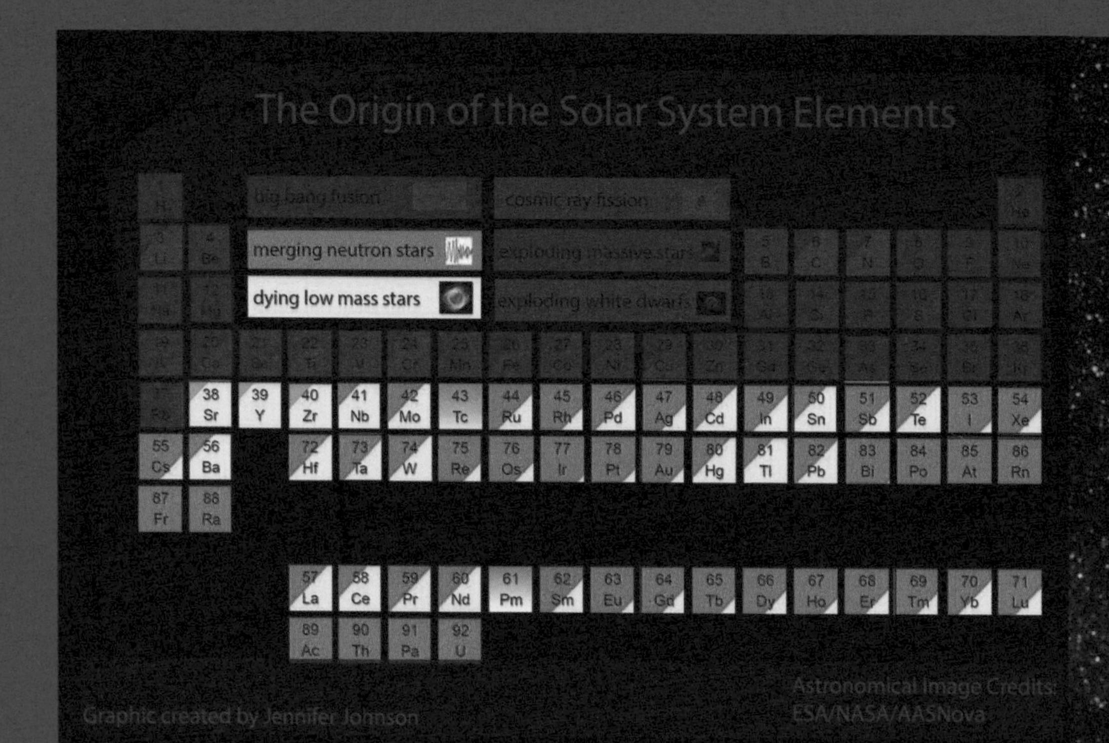

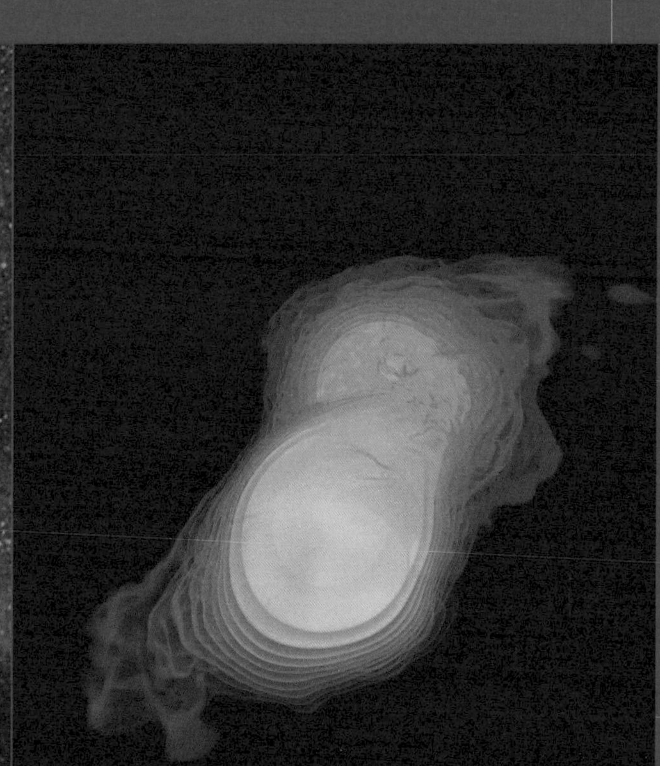

+ *CW Leo, a dying low mass star in a photo from NASA (Wikimedia Commons).*

+ *A computer simulation of two colliding neutron stars by NASA (Wikimedia Commons).*

This rendered view from a hypothetical planet within the Milky Way galaxy 10 billion years ago shows "the heavens ablaze with a firestorm of star birth; glowing pink clouds of hydrogen gas harbour countless newborn stars, and the bluish-white hue of young star clusters litter the landscape."

The youthful Milky Way in an illustration by NASA, ESA, and Z. Levay (STScI) (Wikimedia Commons).

SCIENCE

Exploding meteor over Pittsburgh was equivalent to 30 tons of TNT, NASA says

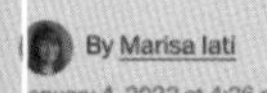

By Marisa Iati

January 4, 2022 at 4:26 p.m. EST

https://www.washingtonpost.com/scie

How a Tiny Asteroid Strike May Save Earthlings From City-Killing Space Rocks

An asteroid hunter detected the small object two hours before it crashed into the sea near Greenland, a sign of the growing sophistication of NASA's planetary defense system.

https://www.nytimes.com/2022/03/21/science/nasa-asteroid-strike.

Christie's Auction House Offers 29-Pound Hunk of Moon for $2.5 Million

The rock crash-landed in the Sahara Desert after a presumed collision chipped it off the lunar surface

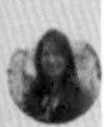

Katherine J. Wu
Correspondent
May 5, 2020

Asteroids still fall to Earth.

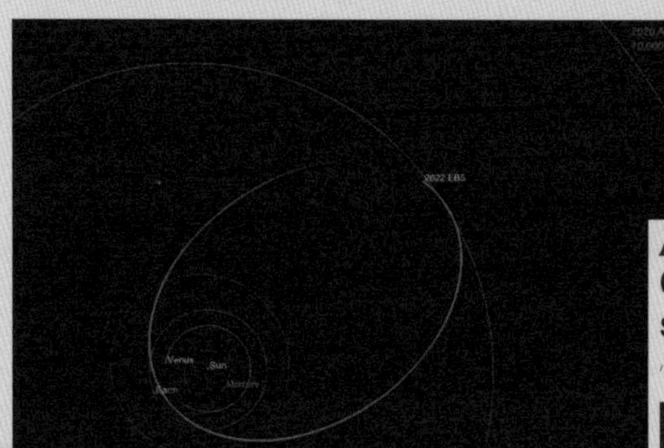

A meteorite found in the Sahara Desert, valued at more than $2.5 million. Christie's

Christie's auction: Kennel hit by meteorite goes on sale

Jonathan Amos
Science correspondent
@BBCAmos

23 February

In total, 602g of Winchcombe meteorite were recovered. This sale fragment is 18g

The Winchcombe meteorite is regarded scientifically as the most important meteorite ever to be recovered in the UK.

It's what's known as a CM2 carbonaceous chondrite and contains chemistry that existed at the formation of the Solar System some 4.6 billion years ago.

The vast majority of what was collected in and around Winchcombe - over 90% of it - is in the UK's national collection, curated by London's Natural

Shepherd came to no harm

A Hu
Offic
Sure,

NEWS

Bri
frag

By Patrick

A

s guide to meteorites

s that fall to Earth are extremely rare and can be
utiful. Dr Alan Rubin, a cosmochemist at UCLA,
, with examples offered online until 23 February

pact the Earth. They are exceedingly rare — the collective
l's annual output of gold.

belt' and hail from 100 - 150 different asteroids. A few hun
); they were ejected by energetic collisions into interplane
ng orbits.

nd — a few hundred million years older than the oldest exi
er than the Moon itself.

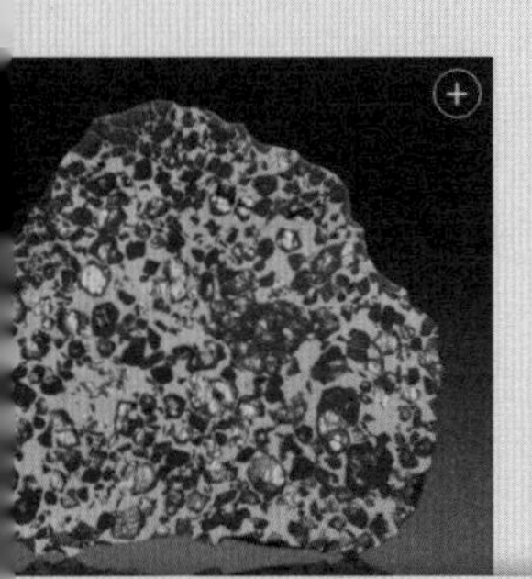

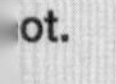

Diamond From Space Is
g on Sale
ot.

WORLD

Indonesian man becomes overnight millionaire after meteorite crashes through his roof

As per the report, the meteorite is carbonaceous chondrite, an extremely rare variety estimated to be 4.5 billion years old and is worth around £645 per gram

FP Trending | November 19, 2020 19:06:49 IST

Josua Hutagalung. Image courtesy: News18 Lokmat

christies.com/about-us/press-archive/details?PressReleaseID=10363&lid=1

PRESS RELEASE | ONLINE | FOR IMMEDIATE RELEASE | 9 FEBRUARY 2022

The Third Largest Piece of the Planet Mars on Earth Lands on Christie's Auction Block

NWA 12690 – THE THIRD LARGEST PIECE OF MARS ON EARTH
$500,000-$800,000

reball spotted as asteroid plunges to Earth

April 28, 2022 | 9:18pm | Updated

ADDITIONAL PHOTO CREDITS

p 58

1. https://flicker.com/File:15516734828_a7bec8ca49_o.jpg

p 59:

1. https://commons.wikimedia.org/wiki/File:Levenseat_Quarry_-_geograph.org.uk_-_325525.jpg

2. https://commons.wikimedia.org/wiki/File:Sodium_carbonate.JPG

3. https://commons.wikimedia.org/wiki/File:INTERIOR_OF_SHT_(ROTARY_DRYER_FOR_SODA)_BUILDING_OR_DRYSIDE_DRYERS_WHICH_REMOVED_TRACES_OF_LIQUID_FROM_STD_FILTRATE._HEAT_CONVERTED_SODIUM_BICARBONATE_TO_SODIUM_CARBONATE_OR_SODA_HAER_NY,34-SOLV,1H-1.ti

P60:

1. https://commons.wikimedia.org/wiki/File:Potash_evaporation_ponds_near_Moab,_Utah.jpg

2. https://commons.wikimedia.org/wiki/File:Potash_mine_Moab_NASA.jpg

3. https://commons.wikimedia.org/wiki/File:Sampling_Potash_Minerals.jpg

P62:

1.https://commons.wikimedia.org/wiki/File: Scanning-electron-micrograph-of-calcium-oxide.jpg

2. https://commons.wikimedia.org/wiki/File: Calcium_oxide_powder.jpg

P63:

1. https://commons.wikimedia.org/wiki/File: File:Production_site_for_sodium_carbonate_near_Dombasle-sur-Meurthe_France_(19630816513).jpg

2. https://commons.wikimedia.org/wiki/File:Magnesium_oxide_sample.jpg

P64:

1. https://en.wikipedia.org/wiki/File:B2O3powder.JPG

2. https://commons.wikimedia.org/wiki/File:Lead_powder_burning_(5).JPG

P65:

1. https://commons.wikimedia.org/wiki/File:Aluminium_oxide_A.jpg

2. https://commons.wikimedia.org/wiki/File:AluminumFromClay_005.jpg

P66:

1. https://commons.wikimedia.org/wiki/File:Hdpe_pipe_installation.jpg

P68:

1. https://commons.wikimedia.org/wiki/File:Bonding_HDPE_for_DX_Groundwater_Treatment_Facility_(7582956094).jpg

P69:

1. https://en.wikipedia.org/wiki/File:Failedrope1.jpg

2. https://en.wikipedia.org/wiki/File:Textielmuseum-cabinet-03.jpg

P70:

1. https://commons.wikimedia.org/wiki/File:Largediapvc.jpg

P71:

1. https://en.wikipedia.org/wiki/File:Laying_sewer_hi_res_(2).jpg

2. https://en.wikipedia.org/wiki/File:Expanded_polystyrene_foam_dunnage.jpg

P72:

1. https://en.wikipedia.org/wiki/File:1937_1952_Prof_Otto_Bayer_Polyurethan.jpg

P73:

1. https://commons.wikimedia.org/wiki/File:Spray_Polyurethane_Foam_Application.jpg

2. https://commons.wikimedia.org/wiki/File:Elastogran_schaumpilz.jpg

P84:

1. https://commons.wikimedia.org/wiki/File:US_Navy_110202-N-2218S-061_Seabees_install_a_sheet_rock_panel_at_a_construction_site.jpg

P85:

1. https://commons.wikimedia.org/wiki/File:FEMA_-_23607_-_Photograph_by_Sally_Mendzela_taken_on_04-05-2006_in_Mississippi.jpg

2. https://commons.wikimedia.org/wiki/File:Gipsokarton-volma_production.jpg

P89:

1. https://commons.wikimedia.org/wiki/File:Energetically_Modified_Cement_(EMC)_Lule%C3%A5_Sweden_08_2020.jpg

P91:

1. https://commons.wikimedia.org/wiki/File:Bauxite_Jamaica_1984.jpg

P93:

1. https://commons.wikimedia.org/wiki/File:Above_the_construction_work,_the_aggregate_storage_pile_1a35246v.jpg

P95:

1. https://commons.wikimedia.org/wiki/File:FEMP_02_154_(27660669640).jpg

P105:

1. https://commons.wikimedia.org/wiki/File:Sandakan_Sabah_Plywood-Factory-50.jpg

P135: http://Flickr.com/File:15036883669_9ebd75e104_5k.jpg

P229:

1. https://commons.wikimedia.org/wiki/File:Limestone_quarry_near_Orosei.jpg

2. https://commons.wikimedia.org/wiki/File:White_limestone_quarries.jpg

3. https://commons.wikimedia.org/wiki/File:-2021-01-08_Men_pouring_concrete_footings,_Trimingham,_Norfolk.JPG

P231:

1. https://flickr.com/File:42294384595_26862c53c0_o.jpg

2. https://commons.wikimedia.org/wiki/File:Copper-199953.jpg

P233:

1. https://commons.wikimedia.org/wiki/File:01-2007-TronaPinnacles-tufacloseup.jpg

2. https://commons.wikimedia.org/wiki/File:Trona_-_USGS_Mineral_Specimens_1116.jpg

P235:

1. https://commons.wikimedia.org/wiki/File:Magnesite_Mines.jpg

2. https://commons.wikimedia.org/wiki/File:Magnesite_of_Salem.jpg

3. https://en.wikipedia.org/wiki/File:-2021-01-08_Men_pouring_concrete_footings,_Trimingham,_Norfolk.JPG

P237:

1. https://flicker.com/File:42294384595_26862c53c0_o.jpg

2. https://commons.wikimedia.org/wiki/File:Interior_rio_turbio.jpg

P240:

1. https://en.wikipedia.org/wiki/File:Nursery_of_New_Stars_-_GPN-2000-000972.jpg

P248:

1. https://commons.wikimedia.org/wiki/File:Element_Origins.jpg

P245:

1. https://commons.wikimedia.org/wiki/File:Ring_nebula.png

2. https://commons.wikimedia.org/wiki/File:Wolf_rayet2.jpg

P247:

1. https://commons.wikimedia.org/wiki/File:CW_Leonis_UV_(cropped).jpg

2. https://commons.wikimedia.org/wiki/File:NS_binary_merger_simulation_153.tif

P248-249

1. https://en.wikipedia.org/wiki/File:A_firestorm_of_star_birth_(artist%E2%80%99s_illustration).jpg

We did not strive to maximize the information that is available, which is infinite, but to assemble a slice of that information that is wide enough to challenge narrowly defined disciplinary limits, but not too large as to be lost into the abyss of an encyclopedia. Our objective is to defamiliarize the house, not to over-code it with information.

There is no Archimedean point by which one can understand the modernity of 'architecture.' Not in the history of its aesthetics, materials, labor, or even in its self-professed critiques. And yet a building as it stands in the landscape is not a contradiction. On the contrary, it speaks unambiguously. But about what? The more one studies it, or - better stated, fights against its foreclosures - the more one realizes it has an almost magical place in contemporary culture. But if in one breath it is magical, in the next it is scandalous.

We think we are designers, authors of note, with agency. But our agency is emplaced - and nominally enabled - by a complex pre-history that stretches millions of years, engages a vast array of industrial processes and complex social and cultural forces that puts the entire earth into play in ways that are well beyond our comprehension.

What is it that architecture masks? That is the question with a thousand answers.

Knowledge must go through the process of paranoiac reflection. Acquired through the unperceived and naturalized ‘liberations’ of modernity its ‘certainty’ comes into view, and confirms self-recognition as a primordial misidentification with control and mastery. Paranoiac knowledge must by necessity lead to a persecutory anxiety and self-alienation that accepts that ‘the real’ is the unknown and that the unknowable has its own powerful platform of agency.

What is the backstory of a house?

OUR: Office of (Un)Certainty Research deconstructed a single, modest, modernist house located in Seattle, USA to better locate, describe, and understand architecture's indeterminate place on the earth and its planetary origins and impact. Four registers, each a type of consciousness, organize the text:

Atomic Consciousness

extending back to the Big Bang and the earliest supernovas

Production Consciousness

a vast array of ingredients to make architectural products

Labor Consciousness

multilayered and global in reach

Source Consciousness

digging into the earth and chopping the forests

Based on the O(U)R research station: Many Houses Many Worlds (out of competition) at the Biennale Architettura 2020, HOW WILL WE LIVE TOGETHER? curated by Hashim Sarkis.

A House Deconstructed
OFFICE OF (UN)CERTAINTY RESEARCH

OUR: Office of (Un)Certainty Research is a design research practice dedicated to rethinking architecture in terms of the emergent scientific, social and political parameters of the 21st century.
https://www.officeofuncertaintyresearch.org

Published by
Actar Publishers, New York, Barcelona
www.actar.com

Authors
Mark Jarzombek
Vikramaditya Prakash

Graphic Design
Angelica Marie Door

Copy editing and proofreading
Daniel E. Coslett

Printing and binding
Arlequin SL

Distribution
Actar D, Inc. New York, Barcelona.

New York
440 Park Avenue South, 17th Floor
New York, NY 10016, USA
T+1 2129662207
salesnewyork@actar-d.com

Barcelona
Roca i Batlle 2
08023 Barcelona, Spain
T+34 933 282 183
eurosales@actar-d.com

Indexing
English ISBN: 978-1-63840-052-3
Library of Congress Control Number: 2022943616

Printed in Spain

Publication date: January 2023